FROM LAST TO FIRST!

10 LIFE-CHANGING STEPS TO NEW WEALTH AND SUCCESS

Humanix Books
www.humanixbooks.com

Humanix Books

From Last to First: 10 Life-Changing Steps to New Wealth and Success
Copyright © 2018 by Humanix Books
All rights reserved

Humanix Books, P.O. Box 20989, West Palm Beach, FL 33416, USA
www.humanixbooks.com | info@humanixbooks.com

Library of Congress Catalog-in-Publication data is available upon request.

Interior Design: Scribe Inc.

Humanix Books is a division of Humanix Publishing, LLC. Its trademark, consisting of the word "Humanix," is registered in the Patent and Trademark Office and in other countries.

Disclaimer: The information presented in this book is meant to be used for general resource purposes only; it is not intended as specific financial advice for any individual and should not substitute financial advice from a finance professional.

ISBN: 978-1-63006-101-2 (Trade Paper)
ISBN: 978-1-63006-104-3 (E-book)

Printed in the United States of America
10 9 8 7 6 5 4 3 2 1

Contents

If you are experiencing failure in any area of your life, you need a helping hand to pull you out of the abyss you've created so you can eventually achieve success and wealth. I'll give you the help you need, with secrets learned over twenty-five years as a corporate turnaround expert. You WILL overcome failure, and your reward will be the rich life you deserve.

Like a general going into battle or a CEO running a business, you have to be mentally prepared to make the journey from failure to success to wealth. In Section I, I'll show you how to use your mental toughness and innate strengths to do just that.

Before you can claim success and wealth, it's critical to take responsibility for your own life and fate. That's harder than ever in a society that breeds dependence and blame. But it is an essential first step in your quest.

If you are going to not only survive but also thrive from failure, you need a new way to look at it. View failure as your first step on the road to success.

Step Three: Find Your Passion and Purpose   **19**

Finding your true passion and purpose in life will give you the energy and inspiration you need to meet failure on its own terms and achieve success. Here's how to find your own unique purpose. As the saying goes, "The two most important days in your life are the day you are born and the day you find out why."

Step Four: Correct Your Mistakes and
Stop Being Stuck on Stupid   **37**

You can learn how to avoid being "Stuck on Stupid," making the same mistakes over and over again. I'll help you recognize that destructive cycle and take steps to avoid it in your life and business.

Step Five: Run to Fire and Seek
Opportunity in Adversity   **53**

The winners of the world know that the seeds for success lie in every failure; you just need to learn to embrace adversity. If you are failing, you and your life are the equivalent of what those in my business call a TUC—a troubled and underperforming company—but you have the power to turn it around. Here's how you begin to reshape your view of the role failure plays in your life and use my rules for turning around a TUC to move toward profiting from the failure in your life.

Step Six: Play to Win: You Are a Born Winner   **57**

You have the right stuff to win all the time in every situation. There's no reason to settle for second place out of fear or insecurity. I'll show you how to find and nurture your inner Rocky the Fighter.

Now you are mentally ready to begin winning in your life, career, and business—eventually ending with more wealth and success than you ever dreamed possible. But mental preparation alone will never lead you to that high pinnacle; now it is time to turn that determination and zeal into tangible rewards. I'm going to show you how I have used my step-by-step turnaround methodology to do just that.

What is the difference between a person who becomes a billionaire and one who accumulates a few million in wealth after forty years of work? The answer is that at the right time in his or her business career, the billionaire had a big idea and bet big on him- or herself. I'll show you how to do just that.

If you are to complete your journey to success and wealth, you need a roadmap—a proven turnaround or operating model—or you'll never reach your destination. A well-executed, time-tested plan is a requirement for success.

You know now that with the proper tools in hand—including a strategy that Sun Tzu would be proud of and my proven turnaround model—it's possible to turn your life and/or business around.

To Catherine, Sarah, and Elizabeth,
my three amazing daughters, who have been my inspiration,
pride, and joy for the last thirty-six
years, and to all of my family. The things of
this world pass, but family is forever.

About the Author

Al Angrisani is a leading expert on corporate turnarounds and the former assistant U.S. secretary of labor under President Ronald Reagan, as well as an author and business media personality. His decades of experience and recognized expertise in both the private and public sectors continue to make him a sought-after regular commentator on national news programs including CNBC, Fox Business News, and Bloomberg TV. Television producers have utilized his background and knowledge of the economy and labor markets to put economic and financial data into perspective for lay audiences of businesspeople and consumers. He was a regular commentator during the recent presidential election cycle, bringing refreshing intelligence and common sense to discussions about the economy and the job market.

He currently oversees two important companies in the turn-around world: Angrisani Turnarounds, LLC, which serves as an operator and adviser to the boards of directors of troubled and underperforming companies, and the newly initiated TurnVest Partners, LLC, a private investment company focused on investing in public and private turnarounds.

His work in the turnaround/investment world led Angrisani to the development of a proprietary Value Creation Model, which has served as the basis for all of his turnarounds. The model is also the foundation for Angrisani's book *Win One for the Shareholders*, which has become a popular and reliable guide for distressed companies facing turnarounds. In March 2015, the Young Entrepreneur Council named the book one of "16 Entrepreneurial Books Successful CEOs Swear By." The book is a description of his model for corporate change and an exploration of current key economic issues.

Preface

Finding Your Inner Rocky

The famous movie character Rocky, created and played by Sylvester Stallone, is Hollywood's embodiment of going from last to first in life. In fact, the movie begs the age-old question: Does life imitate art or does art imitate life? In this case, I think it's clear that life imitates art.

I especially like to reference the speech Rocky, the personification of a failure who turned himself into a success, gave his son when he was failing in *Rocky Balboa*. In this awkward, unusual, and unexpected art form, he lays out a path of recovery for every one of us who is failing in life.

I'd hold you up to your mother and say, "This kid's gonna be the best kid in the world. This kid's gonna be somebody better than anybody I ever knew." And you grew up good and wonderful. It was great watching you; every day was like a privilege. Then the time came for you to be your own man and take on the world and you did.

But somewhere along the line, you changed. You stopped being you. You let people stick a finger in your face and tell you you're no good. And when things got hard you started looking for something to blame, like a big shadow.

Let me tell you something you already know. The world ain't all sunshine and rainbows. It's a very mean and nasty place and I don't care how tough you are it will beat you to your knees and keep you there permanently if you let it. You, me, or nobody is gonna hit as hard as life. But it ain't about how hard you hit. It's about how hard you can get hit and keep moving forward. How much you can take and keep moving forward. That's how winning is done!

Now if you know what you're worth, go out and get what you're worth. But you gotta be willing to take the hits, and not pointing fingers saying you ain't where you wanna be because of him, or her, or anybody! Cowards do that and that ain't you. You're better than that!

I'm always gonna love you no matter what. No matter what happens. You're my son and you're my blood. You're the best thing in my life. But until you start believing in yourself, you ain't gonna have a life.

I don't know about you, but I can imagine my father giving me this speech. And because we can all identify with Rocky's message, I'm using it to start this book. I believe—in its own slightly awkward way—that it captures the essence of what it takes to turn failure into success, go from last in life to first, turn your business around, or just win at anything and everything you do.

So as you read this book, I want you to see yourself as Rocky—someone who, while facing failure, is ready to stand his or her ground and take on the fight. I urge you to absorb the secrets in this book, which will turn your life into a model of success.

It's time to start creating your own Hollywood ending!

Introduction

A Helping Hand from a Turnaround Expert When Things Go Wrong

> *A bit of advice given to a young Native American at the time of his initiation: As you go the way of life, you will see a great chasm. Jump. It is not as wide as you think.* **Joseph Campbell, teacher, philosopher, and author of *The Hero's Journey***

I'm here to tell you there is a way to not only escape the weight of failure on your life but also achieve real success.

You're stuck. You're overpowered by failure in one or more areas of your life—perhaps a business, career, or relationship—and you can't see a way out. I'm here to tell you there is a way to not only escape the weight of failure on your life but also achieve real success. I know; I've walked this path before you. And if you jump into the great chasm, you'll reap the reward of more success and wealth than you ever thought possible.

I'll Be There with You

We'll begin with a process of self-discovery, culminating in the mental toughness, preparation, and skillful execution that it will take to beat failure. But you won't be alone; I'll be there with secrets, organized as a ten-step process I have passed on to hundreds of businesspeople in my twenty-five-year career as a corporate turnaround expert. (Rest assured that you won't find these secrets in textbooks or on the Internet; it is my own system, developed through years of turning around

> The trick to success is not avoiding failure; rather, it's having in your back pocket the secrets for transforming the inevitable failure into success.

troubled businesses and helping hundreds of businesspeople recognize, confront, defeat, and eventually transform the failure in their lives.) Once you've done the preparation you need to face failure down, I'll share with you my proven system for turning failure into personal and business success and—inevitably—wealth.

My formula for fixing failure began as a system for bringing troubled businesses back to life and, in the process, creating fantastic new wealth. My first book, *Win One for the Shareholders*, was directed to businesspeople who wanted to understand and apply that system to their own struggling businesses. In the process of working with these people, it has become clear to me that the formula can also be applied to individuals who need a guide through periods of failure in their own lives and careers. When things go wrong, so many people who've lost their way need help finding a path into territory where they can not only survive but also thrive.

So I decided to write this, my second book, to pass on the commonsense formula that has given me and many other people the help we needed to beat the odds and defy failure in our daily lives.

No Need to Hide Anymore

Right up front, let me emphasize that you don't have to be afraid or ashamed of failure. All of your fellow humans have failed at one point or another—in one way or another—and most of us at several junctures. The trick to success is not avoiding failure; rather, it's having in your back pocket the secrets for transforming the inevitable failure into success.

Here's another part of the secret I'll pass on at the start. Rather than trying to outrun failure, I run toward it. That's right—I actually seek out failure so that, using my formula, I can identify opportunities to create new wealth for both myself and my investors. Like police officers, firefighters, and military personnel who are trained to "run to fire" when trouble breaks out so they can stabilize distressed situations, I run to fire when failure strikes businesses and lives around me. Then I stabilize the situation, eventually creating new value.

I want to teach you to do exactly the same thing in your life: face failure head on, stabilize the situation, and profit (hopefully significantly) from the experience. Sure, this is a little riskier than taking the safe and easy path in life and trying to avoid failure at every turn. But I contend that it is the only way to bring real change and growth into your life.

Take Responsibility for Your Life and Redefine Failure

To start you on your journey, I'll ask you to pledge that you will take responsibility for your own life. I believe that is the first step toward eventually defeating failure and succeeding in life. Self-reliance is sadly lacking in modern society, accounting for much of the failure we see around us.

Then as Step Two, I'll suggest that you embrace a new definition of failure—one that actually emphasizes its role in spurring success. For example, here's how one of history's greatest successes, Winston Churchill, defined failure: "Success consists of going from failure to failure without the loss of enthusiasm."

Another monumental success, Henry Ford, defined failure this way: "Failure is simply the opportunity to begin again, this time more intelligently." (I love that: "the opportunity to begin again, this time more intelligently." Could there be a better place to begin our discussion of turning failure into a positive in your life?)

And through years of fixing failures in my own life and those of countless others, I've developed my own definition: *Failure is a universal state of life, either random or self-inflicted, that provides life's greatest opportunity for change and growth.*

Here's why these definitions are important. Something that "provides life's greatest opportunity for change and growth"

I'll share
with you the
investment
secrets that—
because I no
longer fear
failure—have
helped me
build wealth
for my
investors and
myself.

should not be avoided. In fact, with the right formula at your disposal, it should be embraced.

Once you have a clear view of failure in its truest form—as a real opportunity for building success and wealth—you'll be ready to build on your own innate strengths to start you on your journey. I'll show you how to find your true passion/purpose in life, avoid making the same mistakes again and again, learn to run to fire, and begin to think like a winner.

In the second section of the book, I'll present my proven system for turning around failed lives, careers, and businesses. Finally, I'll share with you the investment secrets that—because I no longer fear failure—have helped me build wealth for my investors and myself.

So put on your battle armor. You have a great adventure ahead of you. While I can't promise that it will be easy to completely transform the role of failure in your life, I can guarantee that the battle will be life changing. So read on and, if you embrace my ideas, you'll eventually discover that true success is a treasure hidden in plain sight. It's right there every time failure knocks on your door.

I Think I Am Successful; Therefore, I *Am Successful*

SECTION I

Success is a state of mind. If you want success, start thinking of yourself as a success. **Dr. Joyce Brothers**

Nothing is impossible in this world if you just put your mind to it and maintain a positive attitude. **Lou Holtz, head football coach University of Notre Dame, 1986–96**

In my twenty-five years of work with failing companies, I have found that too many people have been infected by exposure to failing environments either at home or in the workplace. According to a number of psychologists I have consulted on the topic, that kind of day-to-day exposure to failure leads to the development of defeatist, depressive attitudes—people are left feeling that they are unworthy of winning and having all the good things in life.

Basically, people will take on the mantle of belief that says they are not good at what they do and that regardless of how hard they try, they are going to lose or fail, so they simply stop trying. In addition, this belief has the effect of creating resistance to positive change and a basic unwillingness to stay the corrective course when things go wrong. The lack of a firm belief system supporting a winning mentality causes a quick relapse into the failing mind-set when the first sign of trouble appears.

Why do you think winners keep winning and losers keep losing?

Literally hundreds if not thousands of examples exist of losers becoming winners by changing their mentality to believe they could win and be successful. However, the one that stands out the most to me is the story of the forever-failing New York Mets of the 1960s, 1970s, and early 1980s. They were a franchise expansion team in New York City and the remote stepchild of the New York Yankees dynasty. And then, out of nowhere, they won the World Series in 1986, earning them the nickname the "Miracle Mets."

What happened, and was it a miracle? I believe that the miracle was similar to what I see when a proven leader with the requisite skills steps up in a company or any losing situation and says, "We are not going to lose any more on my watch." If you read Jeffrey Pearlman's exceptional analysis of the turnaround of the 1986 New York Mets in the March 1, 2009, issue of *Psychology Today*, you can truly understand the psychological and cultural change that transformed the Mets from losers to winners.

I want to share a few sections from Pearlman's article and analysis.

By most indicators, the Mets were, in fact, a team destined to fail. . . . As for experience under pressure, they had next to none. "We had a lot of demons and issues to overcome," recalls Ed Hearn, the team's backup catcher. "But there was one thing we had that turned us into winners: one man who wouldn't let us lose, no matter what obstacles we faced. Thank God for Mex."

In Keith "Mex" Hernandez, the Mets had a leader who absolutely refused to bow down. . . . Hernandez was the guy who paced the dugout while screaming at rival pitchers and who set a positive tone for the team. "Just something about Mex oozed confidence," says Hearn. "It was contagious. It made you need to win." And when the Mets won the World Series, Hernandez said, "Hell, we always expected to win. Always." And they did.

To summarize Pearlman's analysis, the Mets started winning because they expected to win. So they did. It's that kind of mentality that inevitably leads to winning.

Therefore, my first job in any failing company—and I believe any leader's first job—is to change an organization's mentality and culture of failure into one that promotes the belief that winning is not just possible—it is inevitable. In the succeeding chapters, I will teach you how to change your own mentality and—if you manage people—how to be a leader who inspires victory. I will teach you how to convince your people that they need to either win or be carried out on their shields. If you follow the steps I lay out for your mental preparation and then use my secrets for implementing change, you will turn failure into success in your own life, career, or business.

You will be successful because you *believe* you are successful. It's as simple as that!

Take Responsibility for Yourself

STEP 1

Ask not what your country can do for you, ask what you can do for your country. **John F. Kennedy, inaugural address, 1961**

In 1961, more than fifty years ago, President Kennedy reminded all Americans of their responsibility to defend the American dream and stand up for the rights of individuals to pursue the life, liberty, and pursuit of happiness promised in the Declaration of Independence. It was a perfect sentiment for the time; the Cold War and the slow steady march of communism throughout the world were clear and present dangers to American democracy. Communism was the antithesis of what America stood for, and Kennedy was girding us for the fight that played out for the next thirty years. The communist regime in the Soviet Union finally collapsed in December 1991, presaged in history by President Ronald Reagan's now famous quote to Soviet premier Mikhail Gorbachev—"Mr. Gorbachev, tear down this wall"—in June 1987.

Ask What You Can Do for Yourself

A lot has happened in the time since Kennedy's famous inaugural address. My guess is that if he were alive today and giving a new address, he would change it to say something like, "**Ask not what your country can do for you, ask what you can do for yourself.**" I think the president would see the greatest threat to America as the same threat that has ruined all other successful modern societies: the growing complacency of its people living in a vicious circle of dependency on a growing state or government.

I believe that, across American society, too many people have shrugged off responsibility for their own lives, looking to the government to provide basic needs like housing, education, and health care. This not only places an unmanageable burden on the country; it also puts government in the position of controlling individuals' lives and, most destructively, eliminates individual initiative. Think about it: What if the current talk of providing a lifelong wage or universal income to workers losing jobs to automation came true? Why should they ever again look for work? Their lives would be sorely limited; they would be robbed of the chance to carve out their own fates and destinies. This is not the American way, and it is certainly not a route to success and wealth.

So before you start on your hero's journey to success and wealth, I ask you to start with an honest assessment of your own personal responsibility. Ask yourself if you are really taking responsibility for your own actions and future or just pretending to be responsible. Do you blame institutions, fate, or other people for your failed situation? Unless you look inward for the source of your problems, you'll never climb out of the abyss of failure.

Pledge Self-Reliance

Unfortunately, too many people resist assuming responsibility for their actions and lives and prefer to default to government to take care of them because society teaches them to fear failure and responsibility. You may have heard or read this aphorism: "Most people do not really want freedom because freedom involves responsibility and most people are frightened of responsibility."

In a simpler time—when governments lacked the reach to control individuals' lives—conditions forced people to take responsibility for their own fates. While people still feared responsibility, they knew the only path to survival was self-reliance. In today's more advanced societies, it's necessary to make a clear decision to be self-reliant. So I am asking you at the beginning of this book to pledge self-reliance.

Here is the pledge I want you to take: *I am responsible for my own actions and the absolute results of my actions. If I fail, I failed doing my best and will learn from my actions. If I succeed, I will humbly acknowledge my actions and move on to bigger and better challenges with my newfound confidence.*

Taking this pledge means that you will not blame others for your failures and are willing to separate yourself from the vast majority of your peers who seek to blame others for their failures. If you can do this, you will have the strength you need to undertake the climb to the top.

There are examples throughout history and across society of people who have grabbed control of their lives and achieved true success despite obstacles in their way. We'll look at many such examples between the covers of this book, but here are two notable stories from our national history to serve as examples for your impending challenge.

Born in pre-Revolutionary Boston in 1706, Benjamin Franklin was the fifteenth of seventeen children born to a soap and candle maker. Needless to say, there was little money in his family for education or career development. But that didn't stop Ben. At just ten, he went to work as an apprentice to his father and after two years went on to learn the printing business from his half brother James. As he did with every opportunity in life, he made the most of his newfound trade, eventually becoming a successful printer, writer, and publisher. His annually published *Poor Richard's*

Almanac was a huge success on two continents and goes down in history as a sterling example of social commentary and humor.

When revolutionary fervor swept across America's thirteen colonies, Franklin took his place as one of the founding fathers of the developing government, eventually serving as a key American diplomat. He will also be remembered as a successful inventor, with the Franklin stove, bifocals, and the lightning rod among his inventions.

Throughout a life filled with accomplishments, Franklin shunned any help from outside forces; he especially refused to profit from corners of the economy fueled by slavery, which he opposed throughout his life.

The foundation of self-reliance that makes this country great was built on the lives and beliefs of people like Ben Franklin. He knew that America was all about the opportunity to be responsible for your success and failure, regardless of your race or creed.

Another great historical example of self-reliance is Booker T. Washington. Born a slave in 1856, he lived in bondage until freed by the Thirteenth Amendment. At that point, he could finally assume responsibility for his own life and was no longer dependent on the government-sponsored slavery economy to provide him with the table scraps of an existence.

He quickly became one of the most influential African American writers and intellectuals of the nineteenth century, eventually founding the Tuskegee Institute, dedicated to training black teachers.

Washington's life work was proving that black Americans could rise from last place in society to first through a combination of hard work, thrift, and a desire to pursue self-determination with their newfound freedom. Is there any better example of responsibility?

Back in the present, every time I find myself in a new turnaround situation, sitting at the table with the CEO and directors who have dug a huge hole for themselves and their shareholders, I listen very carefully to their explanations of their predicament. Unfortunately, in 80 percent of the cases in my experience, the leaders play the blame game, pointing to everything from the economy to the vagaries of fate for their failures. They are products of today's society, which too often enables this type of thinking and encourages the use of crutches like blame and self-delusion to alleviate stress.

My message to you is that YOU don't have to stay stuck in this self-defeating way of thinking. Starting today, you can make the decision to control your own fate and start on the journey to success. Over the years, I have watched countless people turn their lives around by assuming responsibility for their own success.

Let's repeat the pledge before we move on: *I am responsible for my own actions and the absolute results of my actions. If I fail, I failed doing my best and will learn from my actions. If I succeed, I will humbly acknowledge my actions and move on to bigger and better challenges with my newfound confidence.*

Washington's life work was proving that black Americans could rise from last place in society to first through a combination of hard work, thrift, and a desire to pursue self-determination with their newfound freedom. Is there any better example of responsibility?

No More Fear

| A New Perspective on Failure

Failure is simply the opportunity to begin again, this time more intelligently. **Henry Ford**

Once you've taken responsibility for your own life, I believe that the next step toward surviving and eventually profiting from failure is accepting and owning a new, more positive definition of this most universal of human experiences. By integrating into your life a new understanding of failure, you stop playing the victim and let go of negative burdens like guilt, regret, and shame. I want you to begin to see failure in a positive light—as a close ally in your quest to succeed in your business and life. Only then will you learn how to turn failure into gold.

So let's begin by looking at some positive and constructive definitions of failure.

New Definitions of Failure

Based on twenty-five years of dealing with failing companies, the personal failures of the people *in* those companies, and my own failures, I've developed my own definition of failure: *a universal*

Failure: *a universal state of life, either random or self-inflicted, that provides life's greatest opportunity for change and growth.*

state of life, either random or self-inflicted, that provides life's greatest opportunity for change and growth. Imagine that! I see failure as "life's greatest opportunity for change and growth." How about that for an entirely new way to look at failure?

And here are definitions from two of history's greatest successes. According to Henry Ford, "Failure is simply the opportunity to begin again, this time more intelligently." And Winston Churchill made the same point, noting, "Success consists of going from failure to failure without the loss of enthusiasm."

Winston Churchill, who will forever be remembered as one of history's most successful leaders, was no stranger to failure. For example, this man, who later became the very symbol of military genius, twice failed the entrance examinations to the Royal Military College at Sandhurst. During World War I, as First Lord of the Admiralty, he planned an assault on the Ottoman Empire that he hoped would allow British forces to link up with Russian allies. But the maneuver was a disaster, with ensuing fighting resulting in more than two hundred thousand casualties. Another casualty of the offensive was Churchill's position with the Admiralty.

Throughout his career, he often lost elections to public office before finally becoming prime minister at the age of sixty-two. Besides being largely responsible for the eventual British victory over Germany in World War II, he was awarded a Nobel Prize for literature. He became such a monumental success not by avoiding failure, but by using it as a valuable tool that enabled his success.

Henry Ford is another example of someone who came naturally to his understanding of the role failure plays in promoting success. In the late 1890s, he was one of a gaggle of inventors intent on developing a workable, saleable, internal combustion engine. He was lucky enough to find an investor in Detroit who believed in him and gave him the resources he needed to work on his invention.

But it soon became clear that Ford was trying to be all things to all people, developing a vehicle that had too many hard-to-acquire parts. That made the car too expensive for the average consumer. His backer, William Murphy, and stockholders of the newly formed Detroit Automobile Company dissolved the company after little more than a year of existence.

Ford subsequently convinced Murphy to give him another chance, this time working to create a simpler, more lightweight and inexpensive vehicle. But he balked at interference in the development process from Murphy and other investors, so he left the fledgling Henry Ford Motor Company.

Ford now had two strikes against him, with no one in Detroit thinking his invention would ever see the light of day. But family and friends marveled at the inventor's positive mental attitude. He told people that his failures had taught him invaluable lessons. He had learned that, if he was to be successful, he'd have to create his own process and organization around the development of his motorcar.

To everyone's surprise, he found a new investor who still believed in him and allowed him to work unfettered by outside interference. The results were the assembly line manufacturing process that serves as the basis for all manufacturing in the world today and the Model A, a lightweight, inexpensive vehicle that put auto travel within the reach of millions of American consumers.

In a segment about Ford's failures from his book, *Mastery*, Robert Greene writes, "Think of it this way: There are two kinds of failure. The first comes from never trying out your ideas because you are afraid, or because you are waiting for the perfect time. This kind of failure you can never learn from, and such timidity will destroy you. The second kind comes from a bold and venturesome spirit. If you fail in this way, the hit that you take to your reputation is greatly outweighed by what you learn. Repeated failure will toughen your spirit and show you with absolute clarity how things must be done."

> Repeated failure will toughen your spirit and show you with absolute clarity how things must be done.
>
> —Robert Greene

We can see from the lives of incredible successes like Ford and Churchill that both as individuals and as a society, we should embrace failure as a normal and necessary part of life. We should begin to see that it's as essential as eating, drinking, sleeping, loving, and dying—the whole gamut of human experience. Only when we stop viewing failure as something to be abhorred and avoided will we learn how to take advantage of the energy and experience it can bring to our personal journeys toward success.

As I noted earlier, I bring to this topic personal experience learned from myriad run-ins with failure. In fact, I was born into an environment of poverty and failure, beginning my own life experience with the ups and downs of this universal state. But by learning not to quit on life or feel remorseful about my circumstances and discovering what it takes to "fix failure," I have created a successful and satisfying life.

Failure as a Tool to Build Success

I view my personal experiences with failure as a qualification to both speak to the issue and share my suggestions with you, the reader. It all started when I was born into an environment that made success in life a distant dream. The second-generation son of an Italian family in Newark, New Jersey, my life was steeped in all the ills that accompany poverty: scarcity of resources, access to drugs, crime in the streets, prisonlike schools, diminished expectations and self-esteem—and on and on. And while my family valued education, it seemed impossible to acquire it, given the daily struggle for simple survival. It took me some time to learn that these components of failure didn't have to be barriers to a successful life. Rather, they could be building blocks to a better, eminently more successful and satisfying life.

I am hardly alone in being born into failure, by which I mean entering life in an environment that seems to obliterate any chance for success through negative economic, social, and educational circumstances. In fact, based on this definition, 90 percent of the people born each year in the world share my destiny of being born into a state of potential failure. So it could be said that it is a normal part of being human to learn to embrace and overcome failure. Normal or not, however, it is one of the most difficult challenges of our earthly existence, one that even world leaders struggle to understand and master.

President Ronald Reagan: A Master at Building Success from Failure

President Reagan understood the challenges of being born into a state of potential failure. From 1980 to 1984, I was fortunate enough to serve as his assistant secretary of labor, and for two years prior to that, I worked as the then candidate's campaign manager in New Jersey. From the start, we had an incredible bond, partly because, like me and so many of us on the Reagan team, Ronald Reagan was born into an environment of failure—his father's alcoholism worsening an already challenging economic situation for his family. But he turned these hurdles into building blocks, in his case building a path to becoming the fortieth president of the United States. What a great example of going from last in life to first—ascending to the presidency of the United States!

> 90 percent of the people born each year in the world share my destiny of being born into a state of potential failure.

> There are no
> constraints
> on the human
> mind, no
> walls around
> the human
> spirit, and no
> barriers to
> our progress
> except those
> that we erect
> ourselves.
>
> —President
> Ronald
> Reagan

One key failure the president turned to his advantage was the 1976 loss of the Republican nomination for president to Gerald Ford. In fact, he lost the nomination on the convention floor by just one hundred delegates. When I first met my soon-to-be-boss in 1980—in a meeting where I was offered the job as his campaign manager in the key state of New Jersey—I asked him why he was choosing to resume the fight for the presidency after such a heartbreaking loss.

He looked me in the eye and said, "I learned a great deal in that loss." Intrigued by the intensity of his response, I asked if he could share what he learned. He leaned over and said that a few delegates at a convention were not going to stand between him and his destiny.

Again and again, in dozens of different ways, he redefined failure as simply a road sign on the highway to success and his destiny. For example, his words in the following quote speak to the absolute conviction that all failure can be fixed: "There are no constraints on the human mind, no walls around the human spirit, and no barriers to our progress except those that we erect ourselves."

I truly admired Reagan and wish that everyone could have had the opportunity I did to see the power of his positive mental attitude married to his unique determination to do what was right for America and to fulfill his own God-given personal destiny.

Now that you have assumed responsibility for yourself and your own destiny and are not afraid of failing, let's move on to the next exciting step—finding your true purpose and passion in life. Without this sense of purpose, you'll never have the drive, energy, and determination you need to beat failure and build a successful life.

As the philosopher Joseph Campbell wrote, "If you do follow your bliss, you put yourself on a kind of track that has been there all the while, waiting for you, and the life that you ought to be living is the one you are living. Follow your bliss and don't be afraid, and doors will open where you didn't know they were going to be."

Find Your Passion and Purpose

STEP 3

The two most important days in your life are the day you are born and the day you find out why. **Anonymous**

While the path from failure to success and wealth is not easy, I believe everyone has the potential to be a winner, provided they have the drive and determination to propel them over the rough spots along the road. It seems clear to me that an understanding of purpose and passion in life is the engine that provides the horsepower we need through the journey. President Kennedy said it best: "Our efforts and courage are not enough without purpose and direction."

Never, Never Give Up Finding Purpose and Direction

Unfortunately, too many people slog through the morass of careers and lives that bring them only very limited success and no real sense of accomplishment or true happiness. I believe this is because they have given up—usually early in life—the quest to find their true purpose and passion in life. I have found that, without that sense of purpose to guide them, people tend to default to the most convenient career choice, business opportunity, or way to make a buck regardless of the longer-term consequences. In these cases, they are—by definition—directionless. As Lewis Carroll famously wrote, "If you don't know where you are going, any road will get you there." In other words, someone without direction is doomed to wander aimlessly along life's backroads, never finding their true destination. On an individual level, there's the example of someone who develops an addiction and faces the risk of a life of personal torment and failure—unless he or she can gain the knowledge and strength from an innate sense of purpose to seek help and beat the beast. In a business context, picture how a CEO who has seen his or her company and stock collapse, losing millions of dollars of shareholder money, could falter under the weight of failure—unless he or she finds a new sense of purpose and passion to save his or her company, shareholders, and employees from a devastating defeat.

To quote Churchill again, "Never give in, never give in, never, never, never, never—in nothing, great or small, large or petty—never give in except to convictions of honor and good sense. Never, Never, Never, Never give up."

Churchill understood—as all great leaders do—that if you quit your pursuit of a life purpose, by definition, you have surrendered all control of your life, yourself, your career, and business to the world of randomness and uncertainty, where only luck can bail you out. And it never does!

A perfect example of never, ever giving up is author Stephen King. Back in the early seventies, he was married with two young children and penniless. To make ends meet, he taught at a private school in Maine and sometimes moonlighted pumping gas. Things were so tough that he couldn't even afford to buy his own typewriter, instead borrowing his wife's and writing in off hours in a little alcove next to the washing machine in their double-wide trailer.

But he never gave up, continuing to pound away at the old Olivetti and cranking out short stories to send along to a variety of men's magazines. Thanks to his wife's encouragement and his own iron will, he eventually finished the classic thriller *Carrie*. But he sent it to thirty publishers before it ever made it into print.

Of course, the book was eventually published, and he's gone on to write more than fifty books—all best sellers. Why? Because he never, ever gave up on finding and acting on his true passion and purpose in life—writing.

As I have learned in my career, that kind of passion is a rare and invaluable asset.

The Two Faces of Failure

Over and over again, I have sat across the table from CEOs and directors of failing companies who have great educations, experience, and seats at the table in life but no real purpose or passion for the jobs they are doing. In almost every one of these situations, events overtake them and they fail or have less than acceptable results. Eventually, they are forced out of their companies by angry shareholders and public opinion.

But if you take nothing else away from this book, I want you to remember this one foundational fact: *failure doesn't have to defeat you.* If you are honest with yourself and have a clear sense of purpose, you have what it takes to find your true destination and turn failure into success and wealth.

In fact, there are also plenty of examples of corporate leaders who have faced failure and—because they understood or eventually discovered their purpose and passion in life—saved the business and gained an even deeper understanding of themselves and their talents.

For the perfect example of just such a leader, look no further than the iPhone in your pocket. Steve Jobs is an example of someone who stared failure in the face and went on to not only survive but also thrive because of his commitment to his passion and purpose. Today, we think of him as the king of technological advancement and corporate vision—after all, he made the iPhone one of the most popular devices in the world. But we often forget that his history with Apple was hardly a straight line to success.

Jobs founded his company in 1976 and ran it successfully for nine years until presiding over an unsuccessful product launch. The company's shareholders forced him out of his own company, and it looked like he would be remembered as one of history's dismal corporate failures. But rather than giving in and letting failure engulf him, Jobs went on to found a company called NeXT, which eventually was acquired by then faltering Apple. Jobs took up the mantle of leadership again at Apple, developing the products that transformed not only his company but also the technology industry—and one could argue modern culture itself. (The iPod, iPhone, and iPad are the standards by which all similar devices are now measured.) And because he saw failure as a building block for success and understood his purpose was to drive groundbreaking technological change, Jobs was transformed into one of history's great corporate leaders.

Jobs, as I said above, goes down in history as the commanding general of a technology revolution. He knew his purpose and passion and lived it.

The Turning Point

Each of us wakes up one morning feeling lost and directionless, whether we're dealing with a failing company, failing career, failing marriage, failing finances, or family problems. The question for each of us then becomes, can we fix the problem and find our true direction in life?

Unfortunately, many people never escape the cycle of defeat, poverty, and failure. I believe that's because we are not taught by our parents, schools, or anyone else how to develop the problem-solving tools that can fix the problem—whether the situation is thrust upon us or something we create ourselves.

The process and roadmap I am discussing with you serve as weapons against the cycle of paralysis that everyone suffers at that moment. This turn-around process is an outgrowth of my own personal experience. But it is also taken directly from the life scripts of other successful people who have overcome failure. Without exception, these people each faced a turning point where life or career crises or transitions forced a laser-sharp focus on their talents and life purpose.

As the saying goes, "The two most important days in your life are the day you are born and the day that you find out why." Of course, finding your purpose and passion in life is not a forgone conclusion (otherwise, everyone would do it). It involves a self-examination and discovery process that can be painful and difficult. But once you start on the road to self-discovery, you'll find that it's really not all that foreign after all. In fact, if you follow the signs and signals in your daily life that point toward your true life purpose, the path will become more and more familiar. Actually, chances are you've been venturing close to the path throughout your life and just won't know it until that one moment of intense clarity when you can finally see the road ahead.

My moment of clarity about my purpose and talent came at the age of fifty when, after I had

If you are honest with yourself and have a clear sense of purpose, you have what it takes to find your true destination and turn failure into success and wealth.

The two most important days in your life are the day you are born and the day that you find out why.

turned around the market research company Greenfield Online and sold it to Microsoft for a big profit and win for the shareholders, I was sitting in the New York City office of Peter Sobiloff, managing partner at Insight Venture Partners, the largest shareholder in Greenfield. He said to me, "Don't ever do something that isn't related to solving difficult problems. You are a born problem solver."

It dawned on me at that moment that from early childhood, I have been solving problems of all kinds for family, friends, and myself. While any successful person has to solve problems along the way, I realized that I am particularly good at it. I've always been able to see a problem at its lowest common denominator and craft a simple plan to attack it at its core and fix it—all without any unnecessary drama. This is what a turnaround expert does, and it is where my career took me once I got on the right path to success.

My dad always wanted me to be a lawyer, but I would not have had the same kind of success as a lawyer, minister, or politician—not that any of those professionals don't solve problems! A lawyer must help clients sort through problems with the law; a minister helps cure problems of the soul; and a politician must ferret out and cure society's ills. But these careers aren't defined by the need to solve seemingly insoluble problems in quite the same way as a turnaround expert. As someone who focuses on curing ailing companies, I solve problems that are immediate and critical and that have to be *turned around* before imminent disaster strikes, shareholders lose real money and people lose jobs, and families and lives are ruined. That is who I am and where my God-given talent lies. I love to function and perform when the chips are on the table and it is do-or-die circumstances; it is what stokes my passion and feeds my purpose in life.

Can you answer that question as succinctly for yourself? If not, read on!

Defining Yourself

From the moment we are born, the world attempts to define us by the circumstances of our birth and by the opinions of the people around us. Winning in life and business begins with understanding your purpose and not allowing other people and events to define your success. As Frederick Nietzsche said, "He who has a *why* to live can endure any *how*." That *why* of life is, of course, your purpose. If you don't reach clarity about that purpose, you will never be able to achieve the success and happiness for which you have been destined since birth.

Of course, one theory of existence declares that all events—including the circumstances of our births and lives—are random. Based on that theory, life, death, and all the events surrounding them are chaotic, and our survival depends on our ability to survive and thrive in a chaotic world. Another theory is that we start life in predetermined circumstances, and our journey through life is all about discovering and executing that destiny.

My own life experience and the observations of other successful people make me lean toward the latter theory; it seems clear to me that everyone has a predestined life purpose in this world and that our success depends on gaining a clear definition of that purpose and pursuing it with passion and vigor.

> From the moment we are born, the world attempts to define us by the circumstances of our birth and by the opinions of the people around us.

A "Natural" Sense of Purpose

My hero growing up was Mickey Mantle of the New York Yankees. I could never quite figure out why until later in life, when I understood that he was what society calls a "natural." He had the God-given talent to run faster than the next guy, hit a baseball with unusual power for the size and frame of his body, and hit home runs when the game was on the line. I began to realize that

Mantle had found his true purpose, passion, and place in life as one of baseball's immortals and that I had to do the same with what inherent talents I had. If Mantle had a unique purpose, passion, and set of skills in life that he pursued to be a success and achieve his destiny, didn't we all possess the same? Or as my old boss and mentor Reagan used to say, we each need to pursue our own personal "rendezvous with destiny."

So how do you discover and define your sense of purpose in a way that is clear, honest, and powerful enough to propel you on to success? *It's all about defining who you are and what you do in the most basic terms possible—getting down to the lowest common denominator of who you are and what you do well.*

Let's look at the example of singing great Frank Sinatra. It would be easy to say that he was born with a unique voice and that is what made him one of the greatest, if not the greatest, singer of all time. However, looking deeper into the person, I find that at his core—or lowest common denominator—he not only had a great voice but was a poet and a perfectionist when it came to pronunciation and lyrics too. His innate desire and ability to articulate every syllable and to be clear and crisp and as well timed as a finely made watch are what made him the unique success that he was—not just his voice. Like so many other successful people who made the journey from last to first in life, he married that passion and purpose with an iron determination to succeed. Nothing speaks better to this point than a passage from Frank Sinatra's song, "That's Life." It's especially powerful—and appropriate to my message—when he sings about picking himself up and getting back in the race.

You may be wondering why defining your purpose is a foundational step in learning to fix failure and achieve success. I have observed, both personally and by watching successful people around me, that uncovering that definition is the beginning of a process that builds the character of a winner or successful person.

Once you discover your unique purpose and passion in life, the focus, commitment, and sheer willpower also required to succeed become natural allies and you begin to make your own success. It is a self-fulfilling prophecy where luck never enters the equation except to the extent that you make your own. General Douglas MacArthur said it best: "The best luck of all is the luck you make for yourself." My message to you is to let your enemies call you lucky. Their envy of your success will show that you know something they don't. You will make your success and luck because you know the magic formula. You found your purpose and passion and married it to unlimited focus, commitment, and sheer willpower to overcome the odds and become a personal and financial success story.

As I noted in the lead-in to this chapter, it is my observation that most business leaders do not have a well-defined purpose in life and have defaulted to making money and building wealth as their purpose, when in fact this should be a byproduct of their efforts, not the driver of them. A recent study conducted by researchers Nick Craig and Scott Snook (recounted in the *Harvard Business Review* article "From Purpose to Impact: Figure Out Your Passion and Put It to Work") determined that fewer than 20 percent of the business leaders in the study had a clear sense of purpose.

General Douglas MacArthur said it best: "The best luck of all is the luck you make for yourself."

It seems clear to me that winners set high goals, and they have realized that wealth is not enough to define success. My observation of success in business and politics is that real happiness comes when someone truly understands his or her destiny and purpose in life and can translate it to the lives of others.

I know business and political leaders who work from a well-defined sense of purpose, and their accomplishments have stood the test of time. I'd like to share with you a little more of my personal journey with the power of finding my purpose and passion and the stories of other individuals I've come to admire over the years. I hope these winners will serve as role models for you, the reader.

A Purposeful Search for Success

I firmly believe that it was my destiny to rise above my beginnings and prove that poverty would not define me and my family in the future. Once I was able to prove that to myself, I could then go on to discover my true purpose in life. As I said above, I didn't reach total clarity about that purpose until I was fifty, but from the beginning, I was moving purposefully in the right direction—my eyes always on the grand prize. This goal-directed search has driven me through every area of my life and has truly been an engine of success.

Today as I am writing this, my second book, I'm financially secure, have been a major contributor to our country in my service in the Reagan Administration, and am recognized as one of the top experts in my field of corporate turnarounds. I'm also proud to say that my ability to zero in on problems and find the right fix has allowed me to help countless people associated with the turnarounds as well as family and friends. At sixty-seven years old, I am not the richest, most powerful, or most well-known person on the planet, but I am successful, happy, and believe that I am fulfilling my destiny. I feel like a winner and that is the standard I want every reader to think about and apply to their own life as they read this book.

Let's look at a few examples of leaders I admire, who have been winners driven by deep and often unstated purposes in life. These purposes did not necessarily appear at the outset of their lives, but at some point, they manifested and drove these individuals to a successful outcome and the winner status that comes from success.

A Man with a Singular Purpose

I love to share this story. One of the defining moments in my own quest to understand the importance of finding a life purpose came at my first meeting with then governor Reagan in 1980. I met the soon-to-be-president when he was campaigning for the Republican nomination. I had just taken a leave of absence from my job as vice president of the Chase Manhattan Bank to become his campaign manager in New Jersey. It was early March—well into the campaign cycle—and I needed to get the governor's signature on the necessary documents to add him to the ballot in New Jersey. The deadline was rapidly approaching, and Governor Reagan asked that I bring the documents to him in Lancaster, Pennsylvania, where he was giving a campaign speech later that evening.

Ray Donovan, who later became secretary of labor and was campaign finance chairman for New Jersey at the time, let me hitch a ride in his helicopter from Secaucus, New Jersey, to Lancaster. It was a very choppy ninety-minute ride, and when I got off the helicopter, I said to myself, "This is one bumpy start to my new journey." (Little did I know how far on life's highway I would travel that day.)

Donovan and I walked over to the hotel and were escorted into Governor Reagan's ground-floor suite by Mike Deaver, Ed Meese, and Secret Service agents. I walked into the room and saw Governor Reagan shaving in front of the mirror in the bathroom in his T-shirt.

He came out with some shaving soap still on his face and walked up to me and said, "So this is Al Angrisani, who is going to make sure we win New Jersey." (As an aside, New Jersey in the 1976 presidential campaign had backed President Ford, giving him sixty-six of the delegates he'd needed to defeat Governor Reagan for the Republican presidential nomination. So New Jersey was on Governor Reagan's mind, and he did not want to lose it again. That meant getting to know personally the people who would be working on the ground in this important battleground state.)

Governor Reagan suggested we sit down together so he'd have a chance to ask me about my decision to leave my job at Chase Manhattan. He then asked me why I had decided to make such a sacrifice for him and the campaign.

I responded that our country was at risk and I felt a bold change was needed. For those of you too young or who don't remember 1980, the economy was a mess with interest rates at 19 percent and unemployment approaching 10 percent, and economic stagnation was taking hold of the nation. On the global front, the Soviet Union, the "Soviet Bear," was on the march with an iron grip over Eastern Europe and its sights set on dominating Europe as a whole. The unchecked Soviet Empire had built its nuclear arsenals to unprecedented levels. The Soviet Bear saw America as a weak paper tiger, a superpower that it could push around and toy with on the global stage. This was clearly demonstrated by the hostage crisis in Iran and a failed military rescue plan in the desert, in which the United States could not even keep the rescue helicopters in the air to complete the rescue. America was a mess at all levels, and it was only a matter of time in the minds of the Soviet leadership before it could be either marginalized on the global stage or perhaps even defeated in a military conflict.

Governor Reagan nodded slightly, with his head a little tilted to the right—a signal I came to understand was characteristic of his approval. Then he asked me about my background. I told him about my early years, explaining that my parents, while hard-working, honest people, had struggled mightily to support five children. I shared the fact that my father had worked a variety of jobs, from construction to owning a taxi to working as a longshoreman. And I told him that my mother had dedicated herself to making sure we were safe and had proper religious education.

The governor was impressed with what I had accomplished in just thirty-one years; I sat before him now a Chase banker and his new campaign manager in New Jersey. The moment may have had meaning for him because he too had triumphed over difficult beginnings. Like me, he'd had to undertake a purposeful journey to overcome poverty and rise to such an elevated place in life. Our shared experience meant that he understood I'd had to combine focus, commitment, and intense willpower to find my purpose and achieve success. He knew that this sense of purpose in me to overcome and win would give me what I needed to help him win in the New Jersey primary and general election.

After enthusiastically welcoming me to the campaign team, the governor asked if I had any questions for him.

I did have a question, but before I could ask it, he paused, stood up, and asked, "Did I ever tell you my Gipper story from the Knute Rockne movie?" (I soon learned that the governor loved to tell stories.) He pretended he had a football in his right hand and was dropping it onto his foot to punt. He said that every time he did this at the film studio, he would kick the ball, it would get stuck in the lights, and they would have to reshoot the scene until he got it right. Of course, the Knute Rockne story went on to be a great film and one of Reagan's best movies. (It's also where Reagan got his nickname "The Gipper"—for George Gip, the role he'd played in the movie.)

After telling the story, he sat down again and asked, "What's your question Al?"

I told him that I had just one question, and that his answer would tell me if taking a leave of absence from my career and the best job I ever had made sense. Then I asked him why he wanted to be president.

He looked me in the eye and said, "So you want the real answer, the one that makes all of this traveling and campaigning worthwhile."

"Please," I answered.

Then he gave me the answer I allude to in the introduction of this book. He said he wanted to go to the next round of nuclear weapons negotiations with the Soviet premier, and when the premier told him that American negotiators would have to accept his "take it or leave it" terms, he wanted to gently grab him by his lapel, pull him close, and respond, "Nyet."

It took me some time and maturity to realize that Governor Reagan had described to me his purpose in life, the key element that gave him the enthusiasm, energy, and willpower at age sixty-eight to succeed. You see, Reagan realized—long before it became common knowledge—that the Soviet Union and its expanding nuclear capabilities represented an existential threat to the United States. When he came to that realization, he understood that his purpose was to eliminate this threat and preserve America and its role in the world.

This is the key point here: if you understand what Ronald Reagan's purpose was and the reason he wanted to be president of the United States, you know everything you need to about what made him tick. This is not to diminish his myriad other accomplishments and fine qualities. But at his core, he was a man with a mission to preserve the American way of life at a time when its very existence was being threatened. As I noted earlier, he often spoke about his "rendezvous with destiny." Once he understood his purpose, he was able to fulfill his destiny. More money, power, or public adoration meant nothing to Ronald Reagan compared to his ability to achieve his purpose in life. He was a true winner, and I am honored to have worked for him and to have had the opportunity to know him.

Of course, history has many examples of winners whose well-defined senses of purpose drove their success and happiness. Look to the sidebar on the next page for a few other abbreviated examples to make the point.

Ray Charles

Charles once said, "I was born with music inside me. Music was one of my parts. Like my ribs, my kidneys, my liver, my heart. Like my blood. It was a force already within me when I arrived on the scene. It was a necessity for me like food or water."

The world-famous musician had a very difficult and often painful early life. Add poverty and drug abuse to blindness, and you have a scenario that would have defeated most people. But the musician's purpose—to become a respected and renowned musician—was embedded deep within him. It was this necessity, or purpose, that drove him to become one of the world's most beloved musicians.

General George Patton

To quote Patton, "[People] must know [their] destiny—if [they do] not recognize it then [they are] lost. By this I mean once or twice or at the very most three times, fate will reach out and tap [them] on the shoulder. If [they have] the imagination, [they] will turn around and fate will point out to [them] what fork in the road [they] should take. If [they have] the guts [they] will take it."

General Patton knew from a very early age that his purpose was to win military battles and wars. In fact, he often said that he'd lived past lives as military heroes. It was this sense of purpose that allowed him to win any battle he fought, from the World War II German defeat in North Africa to driving the final nail in the coffin of the Nazis at the Battle of the Bulge. In that famous battle, his Third Army saved thousands of American soldiers trapped in Belgium.

This well-defined sense of purpose gave Patton the confidence and capabilities he needed to go down in history as a real American hero of World War II.

Jesus Christ

Christ is the ultimate example of someone who understood his monumental destined purpose in life. From the time of his birth, he moved purposefully toward the moment when he would die a painful death on the cross—a confirmation that this life we experience on Earth has purpose in itself. In the process, he founded one of the great world religions. Christ knew this and his purpose when he said in Matthew 20:17–19, "I die so that you may have life."

The Taxi Driver or Common Man

I like telling the story of a taxi ride in New York City last year that gave me an up close and personal view of how success can develop from the ground up. It came at a perfect moment because I had been thinking for some time about the fact that 50 percent of the world's wealth is in the hands of 2 percent of its population. You have to wonder why that is and what it takes to start with modest means—like Warren Buffett or Bill Gates—and enter the ranks of the world's elite.

On that morning, I was headed to a TV appearance on FOX Business and was picked up by a taxi driver from Ghana, Africa, who had become an American citizen. When I got into his taxi, I was greeted by an obviously happy man who offered a cheerful "good morning." (Anyone familiar with New York City will tell you that the odds of getting a "good morning" from anyone are extremely low.) I replied, "Good morning," and noticed immediately that the cab was the cleanest and neatest one I'd ever seen (and I've seen the inside of more than a few). I felt like I was sitting in a museum where everything was spit-polished and clean-smelling. When I told him that, he said that he kept it that way because the taxi was "the tree that fed him, his wife, and their daughter."

I asked if he owned the cab, and he explained that after ten years of renting, the cab's owner wanted to sell it, so he'd borrowed $250,000 to buy the medallion. He said that he came to America to make a better life for his family. (Note: This is his purpose!) He saw buying the taxi as an opportunity to further that purpose by providing a better way of life. He said he put every penny of savings into the down payment and that it was do or die to pay off the loan, which seemed like all the money in the world to him. He said he worked sixteen hours a day—or two shifts—through sickness, bad weather, and recessions. (Here's the focus, commitment, and sheer willpower it takes to succeed.)

Eventually, he paid off the loan. So then he owned his own taxi and business, which was worth $500,000 because taxi medallions rise in value. Then his family decided to step up and buy a house. So they scraped together a $50,000 down payment by saving every penny they could for two years and bought a house in Queens with a small apartment in the back that they could rent. They were learning that "cash is king," and over the next ten years, he paid off the house, and in seventeen short years, this immigrant taxi driver from Ghana became an American millionaire. It gets better because over the next four years, he was able to pay for his daughter's Queens College tuition and allow her to graduate without any student loans.

So what does this great man who defied the odds and came to America and became a millionaire have in common with Bill Gates and Warren Buffet? He started from the lowest rung on the ladder, but he figured out that success is a step-by-step process, where once you find your purpose, you use all of your focus, commitment, and willpower to create progress and gain those things that are important to you again and again. In his case,

The common denominator in all of these success stories, and in thousands of unstated others, is that at some point in their lives, people who succeed discover or understand their purpose and gain the absolute focus, commitment, and sheer will to achieve that purpose.

it was a taxi, a house in Queens, and a college education for his daughter. In the case of Buffett or Gates, it was building a fantastic fortune one deal at a time.

The common denominator in all of these success stories, and in thousands of unstated others, is that at some point in their lives, people who succeed discover or understand their purpose and gain the absolute focus, commitment, and sheer will to achieve that purpose.

The next step in your journey is developing the mental attitude and toughness you need to stop making the same mistakes in life and move forward. I'll show you how to stop being "Stuck on Stupid."

Correct Your Mistakes and Stop Being Stuck on Stupid

STEP 4

I'm only rich because I know when I'm wrong . . . I basically have survived by recognizing my mistakes. **George Soros**

What George Soros tells us in the above quote is that we can't be successful without openly admitting and correcting our mistakes. That means using good sense to avoid making the same mistakes over and over again. Unless you can learn how to navigate around the "Stuck on Stupid" cycle, as I call it, you will not complete your journey to success and wealth.

Let's take a look at how the Stuck on Stupid cycle can feed on itself and facilitate failure in life and business. (It's no coincidence, by the way, that the acronym for Stuck on Stupid would be SOS—the same as the distress call.)

In my twenty-five years of working with companies about to fail or go bankrupt, there is one constant that stands out in my mind: the script for the first meeting I have with the board of directors and CEO of the failing company. Their stock has plunged from its heights to a few dollars or pennies on the dollar and often hundreds of millions of dollars of shareholder value has been lost by the time of this first meeting, largely due to the denial and inaction of the fiduciaries (principals) of the company and its shareholders.

Despite what emerges as a dark and dismal picture of failure all around, this is what I *always* hear at the first meeting:

1. I (we) didn't realize the mess we were getting into when we took over the company. The CEO or chairman before me was a real screw-up. (Translation: **Denial**. The company failure is not my fault. I refuse to accept any blame or responsibility for it.)

2. But I (we) am getting things under control, and the next quarter's results will be better. Better days are around the corner. (Translation: **Delusion**. If I continue to deny that anything is wrong, maybe all the bad stuff will just go away.)

3. No, I (we) don't need your help to turn things around for the shareholders and find an exit from our problem. (Translation: **Fear-Induced Freezing**. I'm going to continue to do the same tired but comfortable things I've been doing and hope that—miraculously—everything will just get better.)

Why do the people in charge of failing companies take the positions above when it's clear to even the most casual observer that the crisis has reached catastrophic proportions? I have found that only a small percentage of the people at failing companies are smart enough or brave enough to admit they're part of the problem and ask for help. In short, most people can't admit their mistakes and shortcomings and instead assume a defensive posture rather than painfully addressing the problem.

Why I Use the "Stuck on Stupid" Title

If you've ever faced failure in your personal or business life, you may be feeling injured by my use of the term "Stuck on Stupid" to describe the defensiveness that taints the air at a failing company. But while it's a strong phrase, it really is the perfect way to describe the actions people continue to take—despite their negative consequences—through a crisis. And my use of the term is part of a kind of shock therapy I use to force people to look at the naïveté and denial that have often caused irreparable harm to individual lives and careers and shareholder wealth.

In that first meeting at a failing company, I seek from the outset to help people see that the three destructive stances described above are really self-inflicted wounds. Otherwise, there is no chance they can take ownership of the situation and make the necessary changes. So I respond to the three statements of **Denial**, **Delusion**, and **Fear-Induced Freezing** in the following ways:

I have found that only a small percentage of the people at failing companies are smart enough or brave enough to admit they're part of the problem and ask for help.

1. **Denial:** You did it to yourself because you were in way over your head. Or in my business, we say "you didn't know what you didn't know" when you took on the challenge.

2. **Delusion:** You did it to yourself because you naïvely refused to look at the seriousness of the situation. Your childish optimism about performance and results—in the face of overwhelming evidence that the situation was dire—is a fantasy you used to avoid facing the stark reality of impending failure.

3. **Fear-Induced Freezing:** You did it to yourself because when reality finally grabbed you by the throat, you were too afraid to take the bold, painful, and

decisive action required to fix the problem before it got worse.

Once I've painted the true—if sometimes painful—picture for my potential clients, the room invariably goes quiet as the company leaders begin to reflect on their roles in precipitating the company's failure. While people are generally unwilling at this early stage to admit blame, they are beginning to process the new view of the situation.

Now that they are beginning to look at the reality of failure—usually for the first time—I take the corporate leaders back to the first of the three destructive stances and explain that they originally got into the mess they're in by failing to gain a clear understanding of their true purpose and passion in life. That failure led them to take on jobs and roles that really didn't suit them at all.

These corporate leaders facing failure, while they may have had the best of intentions, didn't have the orientation, knowledge, or skills to undertake their current situations and properly react to the circumstances surrounding them. **They overreached!** Then rather than admitting that and facing failure head on, they grasped at the straws of denial, delusion, and fear-induced freezing again and again and again—setting the Stuck on Stupid cycle firmly in motion.

Reckless Overreaching = Denial = Delusion = Fear/Freezing = Denial, and On and On and On

Rest assured that you're not alone in finding yourself caught in the Stuck on Stupid cycle; it happens again and again when people face job or personal crises for which they are ill-suited—when they've reached beyond their knowledge or skill levels to take on those jobs or roles. In fact, I believe the defense mechanisms that make up the cycle are built into our very DNA.

Let's delve a little deeper into the psychology of failure and why people deploy the three defensive mechanisms of denial, delusion, and fear-induced freezing.

Suspension of Disbelief

Almost universally, failing executives' reactions to crisis are to defend past actions, postponing taking the required action until a situation reaches crisis proportions. After years of struggling with the question of why such smart people don't take action as soon as the problem surfaces and get out ahead of it, I have concluded that this is an example of suspension of disbelief.

The concept of willing suspension of disbelief is usually used to refer to an author's ability to make a piece of fiction seem plausible—no matter how fantastic its theme or setting—so that a reader is willing to be carried away on the wings of the story. The phrase was first coined by writer Samuel Taylor Coleridge in 1817 with the publication of a book of lyrical poems.

Similarly, executives at failing companies are being carried away by works of fiction of their own making. They are suspending critical thinking faculties, opting to believe the unbelievable, and sacrificing realism and logic for the sake of promoting their need to feel good. As Sigmund Freud would have said, they are taking the usual human route of choosing pleasure over pain until the fantasy totally collapses.

Denial and Delusion

If we fail to successfully manage our tendencies to overreach and then suspend our disbelief to avoid painful truths, we find ourselves deep in the twin territories of Denial and Delusion. First, we deny our own role in creating the situation, then delude ourselves into believing things aren't as bad as they seem. Delusion is rooted in fantasy; if left

> If we fail to successfully manage our tendencies to overreach and then suspend our disbelief to avoid painful truths, we find ourselves deep in the twin territories of Denial and Delusion.

unchecked and unmanaged, it is a foundational pillar in business failure.

A good definition of delusion comes from psychologist Karl Jaspers. To paraphrase, he said delusion is a belief that is held with strong conviction despite superior evidence to the contrary.

A good example of how denial and delusion ruined a company and many careers is Lehman Brothers through the economic crash of 2008. Many books and reports have been written on this subject, and all come to the same conclusion: the leadership of Lehman was in denial and delusional in assessing their own company and its place in the macroeconomic events that were creating a perfect storm of failure. In his book *Lehman Brothers Dance with Delusion: Wrestling Wall Street*, Stanley J. Dziedzic Jr., a former Lehman managing director, notes that the Lehman management team—including chief executive Richard Fuld—refused to face the fact that overleveraging made the company extremely vulnerable to a financial crisis.

Barry Ritholtz, a financial services expert and commentator, said in his article "The Dick Fuld Denial" on the website Bloomberg View that "Lehman Brothers lacked sufficient capital. It used an excessive amount of leverage . . . about forty to one debt to equity . . . to chase profit in all manner of exotic mortgage-backed securities." Believe it or not, Fuld to this day is in denial and refuses to accept responsibility for his company's failure. This is a glaring example of how denial and delusion can lead to dire consequences. Think about it: no one ever expected that an enterprise the size of Lehman Brothers would fail. But denial and delusion can be so strong that they can sink even seemingly invulnerable businesses. Clearly, Fuld had recklessly overreached and did not know what he did not know about the risks and damage that overleveraging Lehman Brothers could do to his company. In my opinion, if a realist and admitted self-critic of himself like George Soros had been running Lehman Brothers, it never would have collapsed.

The Deep Freeze

The final component in the Stuck on Stupid cycle is fear-induced freezing, when reality finally hits and you have one final chance to fix the problem, usually in an emerging crisis. To be more accurate about it, freezing up at the moment of crisis is a combination of psychological syndromes like conflict avoidance, cognitive dissonance, paralysis by analysis, and so on. But however you refer to the problem, it's always accompanied by a sometimes subconscious acceptance of failure or the belief that failure is survivable. I think this is akin to people who believe a nuclear war is winnable; this is not rooted in reality.

Leaders who rationalize away failure are always eventually fired. In the turnaround world where I live, "freezers" are fired right before the bank shuts down the company's line of credit, when one of the stock exchanges calls and begins to discuss delisting the company, or before one of the leading institutional investors brings out the big guns and lawsuits start flying. I call this the *capitulation event*; it's the moment when people who are not frozen begin to make serious changes. At this point, they usually hire someone like me to come in to try to salvage the situation, avoid a bankruptcy, and improve shareholder value.

> I call this the *capitulation event*; it's the moment when people who are not frozen begin to make serious changes.

History is filled with freezers who have destroyed companies and lost armies and even nations. Here are three such examples that come to mind.

How about Roman general Quinctilius Varus, who was sent by the then Roman emperor to crush the German rebellion in 9 AD? General Varus, a product of nepotism in a Roman Empire in the early stages of decline, led his men into the heavily wooded Teutoburg Forest, where the German rebels were lying in wait. Varus was not only over his head from a military perspective; he was also delusional, thinking the Roman army was invincible. So he and his men ambled through the forest. Needless to say, the German rebels attacked. Reality overcame delusion as Varus watched his men being slaughtered, and he panicked. Instead of taking his losses and fighting his way backward and out of the forest the way he came in, Varus froze and stood his ground while the Germans slaughtered his entire army. In that battle, Rome lost one-tenth of its legions and was irreparably damaged. It was one big nail in the coffin of Rome's eventual collapse.

Then there's Eastman Kodak CEO Walter B. Fallon, who froze in the face of the digital camera revolution. The changing market disrupted his company and business model, and by all accounts, he did nothing to react or counter the attack of the digital camera. And are you ready for this? Kodak's own engineer, Steve Sasson, had developed the first digital camera in 1975. Fallon clearly was in over his head and delusional that the digital era wasn't going to disrupt his nice little business at Kodak, and then he panicked in a crisis and did nothing. All that occurred despite having a technology in-house that would have allowed him to respond or counterattack. He was clearly the wrong man for the job at Kodak.

Ducking to Avoid Reality

President George W. Bush is an unfortunate example of a leader who let failure engulf him and eventually froze. I believe that, in the end, the abyss of the Iraq War consumed him and his presidency. But his problems actually began when he overreached for a role for which he was totally unprepared. If it hadn't been for the tragedy of the Iraq War, he might even have pulled off a mediocre presidency. But Iraq *did* happen, so there he was, caught in the Stuck on Stupid cycle of denial, delusion, and fear-induced freezing.

The perfect metaphor for what happened to the president happened at the now infamous press conference in Iraq, where an Iraqi reporter took off his shoe and threw it at the president of the United States. All President Bush could do was duck. Like the defensive CEOs I described above, Bush had lost his personal power and could only *duck* to try to avoid problems that threatened to engulf him. How did it happen that the president was stuck in this vicious cycle of failure?

Bush was born into a wealthy family with nearly everything in life handed to him, including his political career and a brief business career as the owner of a professional baseball team. He never had to learn about life at the School of Hard Knocks. So unlike someone who starts at the bottom and has to struggle to climb the ladder of life, he never learned how to think critically and determine where his true talents and passions lay. Through most of his life, he performed with the safety net of his patrician family to catch him if he fell. That meant he never had to worry about staring into the abyss and never learned how to assess a major crisis and forge the right solution. He was totally unprepared to face a monumental decision like whether or not to invade Iraq. Because of his lack of experience, he naïvely chose to go ahead with the invasion, all the while fatally unaware he was *overreaching* beyond his abilities to manage the vagaries of war.

Unfortunately, Bush's experience had taught him that if anything went wrong in his life, someone or something would be there to bail him out. But this time, there was no safety net; the Iraq War was not the quick victory he was promised by his generals and staff. To the president's dismay, the Iraqi military did not lay down its weapons in

Like the defensive CEOs I described above, Bush had lost his personal power and could only *duck* to try to avoid problems that threatened to engulf him.

response to the "shock and awe" display of American military power. Instead, the conflict stretched into months and years, and it eventually morphed into a guerrilla war that was all too familiar to an American public with no appetite for fighting another Vietnam War.

Compare Bush's legacy to that of Franklin Delano Roosevelt, who also started life with a diamond-studded spoon in his mouth. Like Bush, he was bailed out of one scrape after another—FDR by a doting mother—in his early years. But Roosevelt entered public service when still in his twenties and had to learn how to deal with the many travails that come along with elected office, including loss of elections, public criticism, and failed attempts to gain passage of legislation. Then he was struck with polio and fought a courageous battle against the crippling disease for the rest of his life. Through that struggle, he learned the true meaning of distress and how painful horrible mistakes can become. These mistakes and bad fortune had prepared him for the challenges of the Great Depression and World War II.

Bush had no such preparation to forge in his mind lessons learned from adversity. While most of us manage to avoid failure as public as Bush's, many of us have ducked to avoid a metaphorical shoe at one point or another in our lives. Here's how it happens: maybe you oversold yourself into a job that you could not do and failed. Then you took another job just like the first and did it over and over, always underperforming. Eventually, you were unable to get a job in that field and had to change careers. Or perhaps you bought a big, expensive house that you really couldn't afford, creating unbearable financial pressure. Then again, it might have been in the relationship department where you overreached, marrying before you were really ready and then facing the trauma and expense of divorce.

In each of these cases, you set yourself up for failure by recklessly overreaching. You put yourself in a position to fail by accepting a challenge with an unreasonably high degree of risk, and then when things went wrong, you denied and did not fix the problem. At that moment, you were Stuck on Stupid. Let me be clear that I am not against calculated risks. We all do it. The point I am making is if and when things go wrong, stop, admit you made a mistake, and fix it.

The Overreacher Personality

If you can identify with any of the examples above, you are probably someone with the tendency to overreach, taking on challenges you are not ready for in life. (Don't get me wrong; there's nothing wrong with aiming high to grow and build a better life. In fact, we'll look at the importance of aiming high in the next chapter. It's when you aim *too* high or far outside your experience, knowledge, and skill set that you're apt to get into trouble.)

If you often find yourself in the Stuck on Stupid cycle, chances are you have the following traits:

1. A natural tendency to be an overachiever and overreach for a better life.

2. A personality that can be delusional in the face of failure, denying reality.

3. A behavioral tendency to freeze in the face of crisis and failure, leading to repetitive mistakes and bad decisions.

Learning from My "Stuck on Stupid" Experience

Early in my life I, like you, had a tendency to overreach. People have told me I was a born overachiever. I was determined to dig my way out of Newark, New Jersey, and become an instant success.

That drive did serve me well, leading to a position as vice president of Chase Manhattan Bank at thirty-one. Then I was tapped to be assistant secretary of labor for President Reagan. I thought I was on a roll!

After the stint with the Reagan Administration, I left Washington and returned to the private sector with the specific goal of making millions. I had read Morton Shulman's book *Anyone Can Make a Million* at least five times and made this my new goal in life. At that time, I had two daughters with another on the way, so I felt a real sense of urgency to make more money and create a better life for them.

So when the opportunity surfaced to join a New Jersey private equity firm and go into the business of buying, fixing, and building underperforming companies, I jumped in with both feet. What could go wrong? Everything I had done to get out of Newark and walk in and out of the White House in Washington had been a success. I told myself that joining a private equity group to make some real money turning around companies was a natural choice for a wunderkind like me, a piece of cake.

The first deal I did was with a small training company in New York. I did know a little about the subject matter, so I was able to figure things out on the fly and improve the performance of the struggling company. It may seem that I was destined for success, but that first *easy* success just set me up for the fall that was about to come by feeding into my belief that I really did *know it all*. In truth, my overreaching was a double-edged sword that could cut very painfully the other way.

The second deal was with a company ten times the size of the first, and it was in financial distress. I had misgivings about the deal from the start but ignored them. After all, hadn't my experiences until now proven I couldn't fail? I was invulnerable! So I let the firm's partners talk me into doing the deal and recklessly overreaching.

You know what's coming: while I was able to keep the faltering company running for two years, it was too deeply in debt and I was too inexperienced to deal with vicious bankers closing in on a kill. The deal failed. I had overreached for what seemed like all the right reasons: I was creating a better life for my family while building a better business for myself and my partners. But I had totally misjudged my ability to handle the situation in front of me; I had overreached, then made a series of bad decisions to cover my tracks. I was deep in the throes of the Stuck on Stupid cycle. I can't tell you how many sleepless nights and hours I spent in denial and deluding myself that things would get better.

First, I was in denial. Despite the fact that the company had too much debt to make the deal successful, I convinced myself I could make it work. I was denying the reality of being overleveraged, like Dick Fuld did at Lehman.

Then denial turned to delusion, as my partners and I made decisions based on the situation as we would like it to be, not as it really was. We made every wrong decision possible, including having the partners kick in more equity to feed our denial and delusion.

Finally, as things got worse and worse—and I was waking up in the middle of the night in cold sweats, wondering how I would feed my family if the deal went bad—my partners and I gave in to fear and froze. We failed to take the actions needed to save the doomed deal.

Needless to say, it wasn't pleasant to fail as I did at this early stage in life. But that experience taught me everything I needed to know to avoid the same mistake. So I regrouped for a few years at Arthur D. Little, a management consultant company, then slowly and carefully relaunched myself back into the turnaround business, which I truly learned to love as I became more successful. As I said earlier in the book, I learned that it was my purpose in life to fix things and make them better. The turnaround business was the right place for me to do that, and I knew I could be successful if I didn't recklessly overreach and made sensible, realistic decisions.

Now at that first meeting with a new turnaround client, I talk about the Stuck on Stupid cycle and share my personal experience with it because it makes the point that we are all human and make mistakes. But I emphasize the need to admit the mistakes that were made before we try to fix them, and to commit ourselves to not

Don't forget that it's all right to overreach as long as you manage risk versus reward, stay rooted in reality, and don't freeze up when the hard decisions come your way.

making the same mistakes again by being a little smarter while we reach for the stars.

As I said above, certain people have an innate tendency to overreach or be overachievers like me. Of those, there seems to be a select group that is able to learn how to overreach and still succeed. In my opinion, they are the 2 percent who own 50 percent of the assets in the world. The question then naturally arises as to whether we are programmed to succeed or fail based on heredity or socialization. It's the familiar nature versus nurture debate all over again.

In this debate, I tend to stand in the nurture camp because of my life experience. I believe that everyone starts out with the ability to succeed if they faithfully execute their life plan and learn how to reach for success while managing risk. As Plato said, "All men are by nature equal, all made of the same earth by one Workman; and however we may deceive ourselves, as dear unto God is the poor peasant as the mighty prince."

I believe that the true differentiator in terms of success is the ability to accurately measure risk versus reward, managing opportunities to a successful conclusion, even while being an overachiever. This formula is a combination of common sense and opportunism. It's a formula that can be repeated over and over again, and the risk can be increased as the individual becomes more successful. This is the reason 2 percent of the population has half the wealth: These individuals know how to manage risk and reward while thinking big. And they do it over and over again.

There are thousands of great examples of people who have come from modest means and managed to build almost unbelievable wealth by wisely reaching for the stars, while knowing how to manage the risk and reward of what they are doing. To avoid getting caught in the Stuck on Stupid cycle, carefully assess each opportunity and be sure that you have measured the risk and reward accurately, wrapping it into a viable operating or execution plan.

Don't forget that it's all right to overreach as long as you manage risk versus reward, stay rooted in reality, and don't freeze up when the hard decisions come your way. To help you avoid the Stuck on Stupid cycle, here's a list of questions to ask yourself when considering any business deal or important decision in life.

1. Is this my purpose and what I am passionate about doing with my life?

2. Do I truly have the experience, knowledge, and skills to pull this off?

3. Am I overreaching, or do I have a way to manage the risk and reward of the opportunity, especially if things go wrong?

4. Do I suffer from delusion, or will I be a realist as inevitable problems surface and take corrective action? Do I have a viable plan B?

5. Do I have what it takes to save the deal, or am I going to freeze in the crisis and rationalize failure?

If your answers to these questions paint a picture of someone who really is ready to take on the challenge at hand, it's time to own the words of philosopher Joseph Campbell: "If you are falling—dive!"

Run to Fire and Seek Opportunity in Adversity

STEP 5

Opportunity is missed by most people because it is dressed in street clothes and looks like work. **Anonymous**

In the past, wildfires were a normal and frequent part of the American West. Every season fires sparked across the plains, destroying old growth, making way for the new, and regenerating the land. But as population has grown, with large ranches and cities and towns spreading across the region, municipalities have aggressively fought the seasonal blazes—with unfortunate results.

"For millennia, fire kept this place a sea of thick, knee-high sagebrush and short grass, patched with clusters of aspen trees. A century ago, the government decided to stop all wildfires. That move upset the balance of the ecosystem," notes a 2013 transcript from the NPR show *Weekend Edition Sunday* about the fire-setting practice in Centennial Valley. In fact, without the blazes, some flora—fir trees, for example—grew out of control and interfered with the natural cycle of native plants and animals.

So now people like Grace Stanley, who worked for the Montana Conservation Corps, actually help start controlled blazes on lands owned by the U.S. Fish and Wildlife Service and the Nature Conservancy to restore the natural balance of the prairie. In the NPR article, Stanley admits that the practice often scares people who live out on the prairie. But she emphasizes that there is good reason to set the fires: "I know that every time we've done burns we get a lot of calls to the fire department, people saying 'Oh, no, why would you do that?' People don't really understand that fire regenerates, and it's a natural process that the earth needs."

Clearing the Way for New Life

That western prairie project is a great image for the importance of failure in your life. While it might be hard work and frightening at first, it is actually an amazing opportunity in disguise. Like a blaze across the plains, failure destroys old unproductive growth and makes way for a rebirth of hope. Let's face it—we humans have always been inclined to stick to what's safe and easy unless we're forced out of our malaise. That's exactly the role failure plays; it forces you out of your comfort zone and into territory where new success, growth, and wealth are possible.

That is precisely why I "run to fire," seeking out businesses that are on the verge of failure. I call these businesses TUCs—troubled and underperforming companies. When a company reaches the TUC stage, it's no longer business as usual on the ground. Old practices that once maintained the status quo are no longer working, and as company profits shrink, people who can't deal with change fall through the fissures in the landscape.

But left in the wake of the destructive forces are those hardy souls who have learned to not only survive but also thrive through failure and adversity. I have found the people who make it through business failures have a deeply ingrained sense of purpose, work hard, can learn from their mistakes, and are determined to be among life's winners. These are the people who will captain the new company on to heights that simply weren't possible before.

In the sidebar are a couple of examples of businesses whose leaders faced the flames of abject failure, only to thrive and succeed in the adversity surrounding them and their companies.

Success Magically Spurred by a Little Mouse Named Mickey

Today, the Walt Disney Company constitutes a global empire, but that was not always the case. Back in the early years of the last century, Walt Disney was experimenting with the new medium of film and struggling to make ends meet. With a partner, he started a small film company in Kansas City called Laugh-O-Gram, which made short advertising films. If the early entrepreneur had been able to make even a modest go of it in that first company, he might have simply limped along on a meager income and retired to a small cottage in Sun Valley. (How different would the world have been then?)

But that's not what happened. Instead, a distributor working with Disney cheated the studio, leaving him unable to cover expenses. Laugh-O-Gram went bankrupt, and Disney was forced to relocate to Hollywood, where his fertile imagination eventually gave rise to a creation now synonymous with animated entertainment: Mickey Mouse. The rest is entertainment history.

Angry and Amazing

In the realm of more modern entertainment, there's the high-flying tale of Rovio Entertainment, a video game company that hails from Finland. No one had heard of the company when, in 2012, its implausibly titled game *Angry Birds in Space* became what seemed an instant success. In the first thirty-five days after launch, the game was downloaded fifty million times, leading to exploding revenue.

But here's the real story: before *Angry Birds*, the company had developed scores of games over an eight-year period. (You've probably never heard of the classic losers *Need for Speed Carbon* and *Collapse Chaos*.) Finally, the company hit upon the *Angry Birds* brand, which proved uniquely addictive for dyed-in-the-wool gamers. Rovio parlayed that addictive quality into $42 million in funding, allowing them to produce all kinds of *Angry Birds* merchandise, bolstering the brand. The marketplace was then ready for the "instantly successful" *Angry Birds in Space*.

> The experience of and triumph over failure is your ticket to real success and profit.

Here's the takeaway from the stories of the Montana prairie fires, the Walt Disney Company, and Rovio Entertainment: if you are failing in any area of your life, don't be afraid of the adversity staring you in the face. Embrace that adversity, run to it, and conquer it! The experience of and triumph over failure is your ticket to real success and profit. In fact, as in the case of the TUCs I turn around, it is the *only* way to spur significant change and growth. Now that you understand that important truth, you're ready for the next leg of your journey of self-discovery—learning to view yourself as a winner all the time and in every life situation.

Play to Win

STEP **6** | You Are a Born Winner

Winning is not a sometime thing; it's an all the time thing. You don't win once in a while; you don't do things right once in a while; you do them right all of the time. **Vince Lombardi**

I am convinced that we all have an inner Rocky the Fighter who just needs nurturing to come out and be a winner.

Of course, there is nothing wrong with finishing in second or third place if you're running a marathon for the experience or participating in a walkathon. But if you want to run a business, launch a career in corporate America, or run for public office, you'd better strap on your best running shoes and decide to break through the ribbon before any of your competitors. Unless you have a clear vision of yourself achieving your goal—whatever that might be—there's no way you can possibly achieve it. Think about it: if you don't know what winning looks like, there's no way to chart a course in the right direction.

It's Not a Sometime Thing

No one makes my point better than one of the best football coaches of all time, Vince Lombardi. This is what he had to say about the importance of always targeting first place.

"Winning is not a sometime thing; it's an all the time thing. You don't win once in a while; you don't do things right once in a while; you do them right all of the time. Winning is a habit. Unfortunately, so is losing.

There is no room for second place. There is only one place in my game, and that's first place. I have finished second twice in my time at Green Bay, and I don't ever want to finish second again. There is a second place bowl game, but it is a game for losers played by losers. It is and always has been an American zeal to be first in anything we do, and to win, and to win, and to win."

One coach who has grabbed a place in history as a winner is Bill Belichick of the New England Patriots. Has there ever been a more stunning performance—on any field of endeavor—than the one he and quarterback Tom Brady engineered in the 2017 Super Bowl? The two megacompetitors put together a series of plays that were—by any mere mortal's estimation—impossible to achieve in a few scant minutes of regulation play. But Belichick planned and Brady executed the plays, threw the game into overtime, and snatched victory from the grasp of the horror-struck Atlanta Falcons.

But never one to be satisfied, Belichick is not content to rest on his laurels. Right after the history-shattering win, he was already looking toward his next win, noting that other teams in the league were seventeen days ahead of the Pats in planning for the upcoming season.

After all, Belichick has suffered the second-place syndrome twice—losing two Super Bowls to the New York Giants—and, like Coach Lombardi, is determined to prevent that from ever happening again. It's not enough that he already possesses seven Super Bowl rings (more than any other professional coach in football history); those wins are in the past. As a winner, his innate fire and passion constantly drive him to look toward the future and grab first place again and again, however impossible that may seem to everyone around him. Clearly he has earned his place as, arguably, the greatest football coach in history.

Finding the "First-Place You"

Here is what I want you to take away from the two coaches' stories: if you are at a place in life where you're failing, you need to reach deep down inside yourself and find that determination to finish first. You need to believe, right down in the deepest place in your gut, that grabbing first place is the only outcome for you; you need to search your soul to find and nurture the winner we all have inside. In fact, success starts one step at a time, so I often tell a struggling salesperson, for example, to figure out how to be the biggest producer for just one day to start the ball rolling. After you finish first in sales one day, then figure out how to do it two days in a row. Build the "first-place you" one sale at a time, one day at a time—or like Tom Brady, one first down at a time.

If I were interviewing you for a leadership position and asked if you felt you had what it takes to always be the best at what you do, you'd undoubtedly answer in the affirmative—that's the natural response. But what I really want to know is how you'll perform when you're faced with the real-life

"It is and always has been an American zeal to be first in anything we do, and to win, and to win, and to win."

—Coach Vince Lombardi

> If, like Belichick and Brady of the miracle-working Patriots, you're determined to win whatever the odds, you are one of life's true winners.

equivalent of the 2017 Super Bowl—when you're down twenty-five points and have to achieve the seemingly impossible to finish first. If, like Belichick and Brady of the miracle-working Patriots, you're determined to win whatever the odds, you are one of life's true winners.

In my work turning around faltering companies, I've found that it's critical to pick true winners and surround yourself with them. At a company in the process of a turnaround, leaders' backs are *always* against the wall, so I need to be sure the people I choose for my team *always* want to be number one—that they are *never* satisfied with second place.

To find those select people, I ask one key question: What happened in your life that set you up for being interviewed for such an important job?

This may seem like a harmless enough question, but don't be fooled. In fact, it is a trick question intended to see if someone found his or her way to my office by sheer luck, by being a safe hire from an executive search firm, or if he or she really had to learn to adapt, overcome, and capitalize on adversity at some point in life.

I usually sneak this question in during the upfront "chatty" part of the interview, when I ask the interviewee *life* questions. For example, what were their interests growing up? What were their biggest disappointments and achievements in life to date? Sometime in the next sixty minutes, I lead them into telling me—directly or indirectly—how badly they want to win, if they know how to win, and whether or not they have the inherent talent and skills required to adapt and overcome adversity. You might say this is my Darwinian interview; it rests on the work of the naturalist Charles Darwin, whose groundbreaking book *On the Origin of Species* contains the following passage: "It is not the strongest of the species that survives, nor the most intelligent that survives. It is the one that is the most adaptable to change."

Too Much of a Good Thing

As I noted earlier, I find that only a select few candidates are stamped with the winner brand. Why is that? I believe it's because many people in twenty-first century Western society have had lives that are simply too easy. They sailed through school (usually on their parents' dime), found their way into a comfortable nine-to-five job, and achieved minor successes without having to struggle for survival—either literally or in the business world. I call this environment *The Participation Society* because it rewards people for simply participating without requiring that they achieve unique success and differentiate themselves from the person in the office next door.

Contrast the picture above with people who've struggled for survival in developing economies like those in China or Korea. In those cultures, people learn early that if they are going to survive and succeed in the nascent business world, they have to work harder and smarter than the next guy, and they can never let up and accept second place. They are the personification of the Lombardi quote that "winning is not a sometime thing."

Another way to look at the issue is through the lens of psychologist Abraham Maslow's theory, the hierarchy of needs. Based on his work with thousands of patients, Maslow developed a five-level pyramid that graphically represents the way we humans prioritize and seek to satisfy needs. The first four levels of the pyramid are what Maslow terms the deficiency levels—and with

"It is not the strongest of the species that survives, nor the most intelligent that survives. It is the one that is the most adaptable to change."

—Charles Darwin in *On the Origin of Species*

good reason. These are basic needs, beginning with physiological needs like food, health, and shelter, moving up to friendship and intimacy, and finally on to the need for self-esteem and confidence. If these needs aren't met, an individual is left with a feeling that something basic is missing in life—a sense of deficiency. Only after these needs are met can someone move on to the growth needs under the general heading of self-actualization.

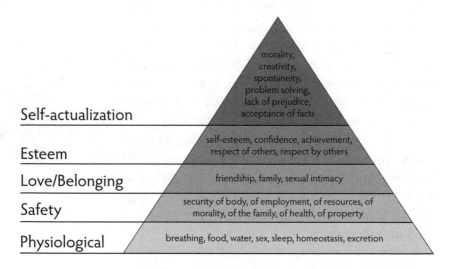

People in developing economies often start their lives in the bottom level of the pyramid, struggling for basic needs like food and shelter. In the process, they learn how to work to win and attain success in even the cruelest environments. I believe that, conversely, many people in modern America and Western Europe live privileged lives, enjoying an early and cushy ride in an express elevator to the top of the pyramid. And because they have never had to struggle to scale the heights, they never learn to deal with the kind of adversity they would encounter in a failing business. While attributes at the top levels of the pyramid are certainly admirable, they are not necessarily the right skills for leading an organization and winning on a consistent basis. It is the bottom levels of Maslow's pyramid—namely, physiological and safety needs—that are more compatible with what is required to win and finish first.

In fact, I believe that, ironically, this evolution into a society that exists primarily at the top of Maslow's pyramid could sow the seeds of our own destruction. If you look at other once-successful cultures that failed—including Ancient Greece, Rome, and the British Empire—it seems clear that they self-destructed because life became too easy and their citizens forgot what it took to win in life and stay on top.

Getting back to my Darwinian interview, I have found that the winners are always the ones who summon up a number of circumstances in which they have taken a "do or die" approach to prevail in extremely difficult situations. In short, they found their backs against the wall, where absolute failure seemed imminent. But rather than accepting failure, they found a way to creatively adapt and overcome failure at extreme personal sacrifice to themselves or others in their lives. They realized that if they failed, their basic physiological, safety, and perhaps even love (family) needs would not be met. Their focus was on survival, and they creatively figured out how to adapt, overcome, and eventually profit from their efforts. This is in the DNA of a winner: the ability to creatively adapt and overcome adversity in extreme distress and with real-life stakes.

Remember the example of President Roosevelt that I used earlier? FDR's very survival was threatened by polio, forcing him to fight to overcome extreme adversity. This was his great teacher, enabling him to win battle after battle for political survival, including being thrice elected to the presidency.

The lesson here is—on a business level—that you should not shun those extreme challenges, no matter how impossible it may seem to triumph.

But rather than accepting failure, they found a way to creatively adapt and overcome failure at extreme personal sacrifice to themselves or others in their lives.

Winners
willingly take
on those
struggles for
survival and
in the process
become
masters at
overcoming
adversity; they
run to fire
and win!

Winners willingly take on those struggles for survival and in the process become masters at overcoming adversity; they run to fire and win!

Real Success Is Repeatable

As my Darwinian interview progresses, I move on to discover if an interviewee is committed to winning over and over again. Unfortunately, all too many people are unwilling to pay the price associated with being an every-time winner.

For example, in my work, I often meet people who participate in a successful turnaround, have a big payday, and opt for an easier life from that point on. After that one big success, I can't get them to leave their life on the beach. They're obviously not real winners.

Another environment that seems to breed one-hit wonders is sports. How often does a pro player have one stunning season, nab a big contract, and then revert back to their norm of mediocrity? They are suddenly merely *showing up* for games, eventually fading into oblivion with their ill-gotten gains. (As an aside, the general managers who hand out these contracts in the first place are often overreaching beyond their skill levels—evidenced by the fact they didn't see the very clear signs that the athletes were not serial winners. They are good examples of the Stuck on Stupid syndrome I described in the last chapter.)

Here's what Lombardi had to say about what it takes to be a winner and remain a success: "To achieve success, whatever the job we have, we must pay a price. Success is like anything worthwhile. It has a price. You have to pay the price to win and you have to pay the price to get to the point where success is possible. Most important, you must pay the price to stay there."

The serial winners who know how to finish first understand what Lombardi is talking about and consider themselves better for having what it takes to win over and over again. Just look at the lives of Tom Brady, Michael Jordan, Arnold Palmer, Jack Nicklaus, General Patton, FDR, Warren Buffett and so many other Americans who have learned to win and finish first not once, but over and over and over again. One thing all serial winners have in common is that they understand that winning is not about the money. Instead, winning is about maintaining a commitment to excellence in their chosen profession, accompanied by discipline and a will to win. It's clear that they take pride in their trade, have the discipline to work hard all the time, and possess the will to endure whatever comes their way in order to win again and again. Winning and finishing first is their real prize, with money taking second place.

One thing all serial winners have in common is that they understand that winning is not about the money. Instead, winning is about maintaining a commitment to excellence in their chosen profession.

One of the best examples of consistent commitment to personal and professional excellence is Oprah Winfrey. Years ago when she started her career in radio, it would have been easy to dismiss her. She was a poor, young black woman from a very troubled and disadvantaged background. You might have placed the odds of success at a million-to-one against her. However, the American legend has been a serial winner across multiple disciplines, including radio, television, film, and business—nearly everything but politics—and she is still relatively young. Her net worth is estimated at $3 billion, but it is her commitment to excellence, combined with intense discipline, hard work, and a will to win that have rocketed her to the top of the list of successful serial winners in modern-day America.

These are the things I'm always looking for when I try to hire and surround myself with winners. I have come to realize that success has nothing to do with whether someone is white, black, young, old, rich, poor, tall, short, handsome, or unattractive. The will to win again and again comes from a place deep inside—their inner Rocky.

Now that you understand the mind-set and mentality it takes to be a winner and turn your life and business around, you're ready to go on to Section II, where I'll show you how to use my proven turnaround model and blueprint for success and wealth.

With This Secret Formula, I Turn Success into Wealth

SECTION **II**

Good business leaders create a vision, articulate the vision, passionately own the vision, and relentlessly execute the vision to completion. **Jack Welch, former chairman and CEO of General Electric**

Now you are mentally ready to begin winning in your life, career, and business, eventually ending with more wealth and success than you ever dreamed possible. But mental preparation alone will never lead you to that high pinnacle; now it is time to turn that determination and zeal into tangible rewards. I'm going to show you how you can do just that, using my step-by-step turnaround methodology.

I can't emphasize enough that the key to my success in twenty-five years in the turnaround business has been the relentless execution of a well-designed strategy and implementation plan. Now I'm going to share with you the art form of creating a win/win strategy and the science behind an effective implementation plan, or as I like to call it, "The Art of the Turnaround." Hopefully, you will be able to use it in your business and life like so many others did with my first book, *Win One for the Shareholders*.

I can't emphasize enough that the key to my success in twenty-five years in the turnaround business has been the relentless execution of a well-designed strategy and implementation plan.

In the chapters ahead, I will walk you through the roadmap for crafting a winning life and career strategy and executing it to completion—in keeping with the great quote from Jack Welch that starts this chapter. And here's why this is such a gift: I can tell you unequivocally that you will not be able to find what you are going to read in the chapters ahead in any business school class or textbook. You may encounter various aspects of what I am going to teach you, but you will not see my unique model and formula for successfully fixing failure and turning your life, career, and business around.

My model is unique because it was born and nurtured out of the singular experiences and challenges I have encountered in each of my many turnarounds. (You might say I'm the poster child of on-the-job training.) Over the years, I've learned how to turn those challenges around and build creative solutions, and I've wrapped them into a proven and working turnaround model. This is critical because turnarounds of any kind—personal or business—are very difficult. According to recent data, over half of all corporate turnarounds fail. In fact, Peter Cuneo, another recognized turnaround expert, estimated in a recent Forbes interview that nine out of ten turnarounds fail. I think you get the point; turning around your business and life is no easy task. If it were, I would not be writing this book about it and would have had to figure out another way to make a good living.

To further set the stage for the chapters ahead, let me refer to a 2014 article by the Turnaround Management Association (TMA) that underscores the reasons companies fail or the root cause of most business failures. Based on a study of more than four hundred companies, the TMA determined that most crises and failures are caused by the mistakes of top management, not product deficiencies, collapsing markets, technology disruption, or any of the dozens of reasons sometimes trotted out to excuse the demise of a business. It's all about mistakes by top management or the decisions made by people in charge. The article notes that the biggest specific mistake made by management is continuing with a strategy that no longer works for the company because management lost touch with the market and their customers. Right behind this primary cause for failure is the unwillingness to adapt to change or the inability to execute a strategy to address change. These are both mistakes resulting from the thought processes of top management, which mirrors the direct relationships in our personal lives between personal decisions and the mistakes and failures we bring upon ourselves.

The survey found the following facts:

- Management held on to strategies that were not working in 54.5 percent of the companies surveyed.
- Management did not want to adapt or could not adapt/execute change in 51.2 percent of the companies surveyed.
- Management had no "vision" in 51.4 percent of the companies surveyed.

These findings are very consistent with what I uncover when I inherit a failing company and work my way back to the root cause of the failure. Incidentally, these mistakes plague leaders and decision makers in all aspects of life. Just look at how Hillary Clinton missed the shift of the electorate to a more populist point of view, then failed to adapt to it. When she finally did recognize it, she could not execute a strategy that worked. What she did is a classic parallel to how management and decision makers in companies fail. On the other side of the coin, both President Donald Trump and Bernie Sanders saw the strategic shift to populism and built strategies to capitalize on it. Obviously, President Trump executed on his strategy better than the competition.

Perhaps the best example of business failure due to bad decision-making is General Motors (GM), the American icon that could do no wrong for fifty years. But the world changed around GM, and managers did not keep pace. From 2000 to 2009, GM continued to focus its core business on making large vehicles rather than diversifying downstream to the smaller, more efficient vehicles that the public was demanding. When the collapse of 2008 hit and the economy went limp, GM and its predominately large-vehicle product line could not weather the storm. The end result was bankruptcy. If Uncle Sam hadn't been around with a blank check in the form of a taxpayer bailout for GM, the company would not be around today. At the core of GM's failure and the root cause of its bankruptcy were mistakes by management.

I believe turnarounds fail due to lack of a strategy that integrates each element of the plan into a model that is greater than the sum of its parts.

In the chapters ahead, you will see that I provide a playbook or model on how to make the correct decisions, avoid mistakes, and take the right steps to execute your own vision of winning. I'll show you how to use your new passion and winning mind-set to reverse the negative momentum of the failure around you and stabilize your situation—inevitably creating growth and new value.

This is an integrated model, with every link in the chain as strong as every other. Therefore, elements in the model function independently and in sync. You can see this system at work in the U.S. military. We have five branches—Army, Navy, Marine Corps, Coast Guard, and Air Force—that function independently but interdependently to ensure victory. If one branch is being weakened under attack, the other branches of the military are there with reinforcements. This is important in personal and business life as well as in the military because I believe turnarounds fail due to lack of a strategy that integrates each element of the plan into a model that is greater than the sum of its parts. So read on and learn how to use my model to execute your newfound commitment to turning failure into success and wealth. It's just a matter of taking one step at a time until the journey is complete.

Go Big or
Go Home

STEP 7 | Negotiate a Big Payday for
You and Your Family

*Better to have and not need money than to need and not
have money.* **Unknown**

What is the difference between a person who becomes a billionaire and one who accumulates a few million in wealth after forty years of work? The answer is that at the right time in his or her business career, the billionaire had a big idea and bet big on him- or herself. If you have been paying attention to one of the central messages in this book—that failure is an opportunity—then you now understand that you need to be mentally prepared to negotiate a deal for yourself with the board of directors, your investors, or the bank that has a big payday when you succeed. Unfortunately, the art of negotiating a big or good deal is an acquired art form and the manner in which you negotiate your payday could be the difference between having a payday that makes you just comfortable and one that makes you rich.

In his book *The Art of the Deal*, President Trump makes three key points that frame almost every negotiation for a big payday from your employer or investors. The book is really an excellent source of information on the subtle aspects of negotiating a great deal and how to come out on top in any negotiation.

First, keep your family in mind when you are applying yourself to your work. While Trump has actually physically brought his family into his business—and administration—that is not absolutely necessary. The point is to recognize that you are negotiating for the future of your children and grandchildren, so to some degree, their fate is in your hands. This thought process raises the bar because while you may find it difficult to be greedy for yourself, what parent does not want the very, very best for his or her children and future grandchildren? In a way, it is part of your purpose in life and a responsibility you owe to your children and future generations. It would not be going too far to view the negotiation for your compensation for fixing a broken business, joining a start-up, or taking a new job with all of its inherent risks as a life-or-death (or at least career life-or-death) situation. So make sure you get paid well—for everyone's sake.

As an aside, I have also come to the conclusion that drawing on concern for family is an essential part of motivating key people to produce and win. And I have developed a unique way to use that motivating factor. For my second meeting with the key team member of a failing business, I include the team member's spouse. During that meeting, I explain to the spouse that we are going to negotiate a compensation deal that—if we succeed and win—is going to be a game changer in their family's life.

So I then ask the couple what a game changer means to them as a family, and I usually get back very specific answers like paying off their house, funding their children's college educations, or funding their retirement. (You get the point!) Based on this meeting, we end up negotiating a compensation program that accomplishes the family goals. From that point on, the turnaround is a family affair. It helps to justify the long hours away from home and other personal sacrifices needed to win. In some instances, I have even had a spouse check in with me periodically to see how things were going and if the husband or wife was working hard enough. So I definitely agree with Trump that the art of a good deal involves bringing the family into the deal, one way or another.

Second, go into a negotiation like it's a fight to the death. You have to be prepared to go down fighting and even leave money on the table rather than take a bad deal. Of course, make sure you have an exit plan, but don't be afraid to raise the level of tension to the point that the other guy has to back down.

Third, think big and pitch big results from your efforts to raise the bar on negotiations. As Trump wrote, "Most people are afraid to think big, but get excited by people who do think big." By extension, people are always more inclined to pay the big thinker than the measured person who wants to underpromise and overdeliver. Underpromising and overdelivering is a great strategy when operating a business but not when negotiating your deal.

There are no better examples of "go big or go home" when it comes to negotiating your deal than the deals of these four executives who were thinking big when they negotiated their deals:

- Lee Raymond exited Exxon with a $398 million severance package.

> "Most people are afraid to think big, but get excited by people who do think big."
>
> —President Donald Trump

- William McGuire exited United Health with a
  $1.6 billion exit package.
- Robert Nardelli left Home Depot with a $212 million exit
  package.
- Henry McKinnel left Pfizer with a $200 million exit
  package.

The list could go on to include hundreds of other smart executives who made hundreds of millions and billions by being shrewd negotiators, in addition to being competent executives.

Another example of shrewd and aggressive negotiating when creating fortunes is in the professional sports arena. How about the Yankees paying Alex Rodriquez $250 million for one championship year, a few other good years, and a lot of distractions? This is a great example of brilliant negotiating by A-Rod and his agent and an even better example of thinking big and promising big things. I am sure the Yankees thought A-Rod would break the all-time home run record as a Yankee and restore an era of greatness. It did not happen, but A-Rod got paid!

And then there is the case of quarterback Jamarcus Russell, who was paid $68 million by the Oakland Raiders, despite the fact that he failed to produce. Or how about Grant Hill being paid $93 million by the Orlando Magic when he only played four injury-plagued years? What about Ryan Leaf, who was paid $32 million by the San Diego Chargers for four unproductive years?

The point here is that the negotiation is as much, if not more, a potential source of real wealth creation than the actual level of performance. This is not to say that hard work and concentrated effort are not important elements in creating wealth. But remember that in the process of working hard, you need to think big and try to find the leverage to negotiate a big deal for you and your family. I call it putting yourself in a win/win place, so regardless of the outcome, you win!

Now with your new mind-set of a winner and a deal that makes you and your family rich, you are ready to play the game and capitalize on the opportunity in front of you to fix failure and create the success and prosperity that comes with it.

The negotiation is as much, if not more, a potential source of real wealth creation than the actual level of performance

The Proven Turnaround

STEP 8 | # Model

> *If you don't know where you are going any road will get you there.* **Lewis Carroll, *Alice's Adventures in Wonderland***

If you are going to complete your journey to success and wealth, you need a roadmap—a proven turnaround or operating model—or you'll never reach your destination. A well-executed, time-tested plan can help you gain momentum and stay the course. This same principle holds true for personal or career turnarounds: you need a plan you can trust to guide you through the tough moments and into the clear light of success.

This became clear from the very beginning of my career during my first turnaround. The project took more than four years to achieve when it should have been done in under two. (Incidentally, since that deal and the creation of my proven turnaround model, my turnarounds have averaged about eighteen months. This is evidence of the power of having a proven model.)

The Building Blocks of a Turnaround

> A successful turnaround is built from the ground up, with each step supporting the steps that follow, much like the cement blocks in a structure's foundation.

After my first deal, I realized how unique my work was and decided to create my own turnaround model. Fortunately, I had good records and detailed notes of all the actions taken throughout that initial four-year turnaround. So like a good detective, I was able to reconstruct the scene of the crime. A few key characteristics of turnarounds jumped off the pages immediately and formed the foundation of my model. (Since that time, I have successfully used the model on numerous new turnarounds, achieving returns for shareholders that well exceed returns for the S&P 500 or any other reliable stock market index.)

The first revelation was that a successful turnaround is built from the ground up, with each step supporting the steps that follow, much like the cement blocks in a structure's foundation.

I also learned that the sequencing of actions was critical; a misplaced block means the whole structure could topple. For example, if you fix sales before you fix sales operations, the company might experience a temporary spike in sales, but the broken back office would eventually lead to lower customer satisfaction scores. That, in turn, would lead to reduced sales and another downward slide.

This phenomenon always reminds me of the story of Sisyphus from Greek mythology. Sisyphus, the King of Corinth, was punished by the gods for his greed and deceit by being condemned to roll a giant boulder up a hill, only to have it roll down and pummel him again and again. He was forced to perform this futile task throughout eternity.

I learned early in my career that I would suffer the same fate as Sisyphus if I didn't build a strong foundation by properly sequencing the building blocks of a turnaround.

This bottom-up, logically sequenced approach certainly holds true for turnarounds in other aspects of life. Those who buy big, expensive houses before establishing financial security, for example, will spend their lives endlessly pushing the financial boulder uphill.

And speaking of financial security, here's the next important principle of turnarounds.

Cash Is King

The next thing I learned was that the new building blocks of progress had to be cemented in place with *cash*. Without cash, you simply can't sustain the hard and risky work of your business or personal turnaround. In my first book, *Win One for the Shareholders*, where I lay out the detailed version of my turnaround model, I say, "Cash and the ability to generate new cash from operations are, next to the intellectual capital in the company, the most valuable assets of the turnaround."

This "cash is king" concept has been a big factor in my personal wealth-building success from very early in my life. For example, growing up poor as a church mouse, I remember the first cash I ever made. I was eleven years old and helped the local paperboy deliver papers, earning seventy-five cents for the week. I took that money and immediately bought a pair of streamers for my old beaten-down bike that my Uncle Albert had given me, making my bike at least a little cool around the neighborhood. It stayed with me that cash was the difference between having and not having and between self-empowerment and no power. I went on to assume the paper route and

Without cash, you simply can't sustain the hard and risky work of your business or personal turnaround.

saved $400 in two years, and I was able to use that money to help my family in a time of need. Again, the power to make a difference came from cash.

At every stage of my ensuing career, I've made myself take one-third or more of my earnings and stash it away in safe cash investments. So I have never been afraid to take a reasonable business risk or help someone because I had the cash to make things work. To make my point even more forcefully, at age thirty-one, I left my secure job at Chase Manhattan Bank to be Ronald Reagan's campaign manager in New Jersey with zero job security. I would never have taken this risk if I did not have the required cash reserves to get back on my feet if he lost. The risk I took there, in large part because of my cash reserves, changed my life in a positive way forever.

This same principle of "cash is king" applies to a business turn-around and the need to create cash reserves early on to sustain a business when things go wrong. A personal and powerful example of this was Microsoft and its huge cash hoard during the stock market collapse of 2008. The world almost stopped, but Microsoft hardly blinked because it had huge cash reserves and was throwing off over $25 billion in new cash every year. I felt the power of the "cash is king" message personally because Microsoft had agreed to purchase my newly turned-around Greenfield Online for about $500 million in September 2008. The markets crashed in the middle of this deal, so I was expecting a call from the head of Microsoft's mergers and acquisitions department telling me the deal was off. Microsoft powered through the crash, however, viewing it as an opportunity to move forward on this and other deals, while other overleveraged competitors were frozen by events beyond their control. In our case, the deal closed and shareholders and everyone got paid and made money.

Times They Are A-Changin'

The last and perhaps most fluid characteristic of turnarounds is the fact that today's new products, technologies, or ideas have specific and ever-decreasing life cycles. Not too long ago, you could introduce a new product and ride the wave of success for three to five years before being challenged. This is not the case today. Now any new product that impacts the market could have a legitimate challenge in eighteen months or sooner. This compression of the new product life cycle makes it more important to determine if a turnaround can be sustained for a long period of time or if the company is better sold to bigger and stronger strategic or financial players who can beat copycat competitors on their own turf.

I like to use the example here of my turnaround of Harris Interactive, founded by Lou Harris and best known for the Harris Poll, one of the world's oldest polling and research companies. Harris Interactive had fallen on bad times as the world and technology changed around it and it failed to properly respond to that change. The stock was collapsing and was well under one dollar a share when I arrived. Needless to say, cash was tight to nonexistent, and talent and intellectual capital were also in short supply. It was a bad situation, and if it had been my first or second turnaround, I would have certainly failed. But because I had more than twenty years of experience dealing with crises under my belt, I was able to turn things around and stabilize the company, cash, and business operations. I told and still tell the management team when I see them that we pulled off a miracle. Because of hard work, the turnaround model, and the grace of God, we made a failing situation a success. I halfheartedly joke and tell everyone that I now go to church twice on Sunday to say thank you for the miracle of Harris.

However, eighteen months from the start of the turnaround to the point where we had stabilized things and the stock had more than doubled in price, I knew that while we had been busy keeping Harris out of bankruptcy and turning it around, the world had moved on. To stay and fight further would have required millions of dollars of investment in the new digital and artificial intelligence technologies coming on stream at a rapid pace. We just did not have the type of money to compete in the future, so we made the decision to sell to Nielsen Ratings, a big, powerful, cash-rich and well-managed company that could take all or part of what we had salvaged at Harris to the next level. It was the right thing to do for the shareholders, the employees, and the business.

Make no mistake about it, your window of opportunity to recover from a personal or career failure is also narrowing in this fast-paced, global economy. Yesterday, you may have worried about the guy in the next cubicle. Today, your job could be snatched up by an engineer from Bombay or Dubai.

The Digital Revolution Has Changed My Turnaround Model

The technology and digital revolution has impacted the turnaround world just as it has every other area of modern life. Since 2008 when I wrote *Win One*, the constantly growing world of bits and bytes has made marketing a central issue in the turnaround process. In fact, new digital and social media means of reaching customers have made marketing an almost one-to-one exercise. Consequently, it is now much more important to the overall effort to use digital technology to drive new sales and revenue in a distressed company. Artificial intelligence (AI) in particular is making new research, databases, and data management platforms available to marketing personnel and creating highly targeted new business opportunities daily and at a fraction of the cost of previous processes to identify new customers.

Another change driven by the new digital and AI marketing world is the ability to bring new products to market more quickly than ever before. If tactical investments are made to improve profitable core products early enough in the life cycle of the turnaround, then the new entries can generate sales and revenue more quickly. This provides critical support and can shorten the overall turnaround process if it is executed properly and efficiently.

Please note that I said *tactical investments* in research and development to improve profitable core products. Let me emphasize again that **this does not mean spending money and time**

creating new products. That approach always fails when the life cycle of the turnaround is two years or less. But a refresh of existing products can pay big dividends because of the new speed of marketing in the digital marketing world.

Look at how entertainment giant Netflix took advantage of the digital revolution to eventually dominate the television- and movie-watching landscape.

Today, the name Netflix is virtually synonymous with binge-watching, that favorite pursuit of millennials. Billions of hours of programming are now streamed across the service every month. But the company actually began life in the early years of the digital revolution—back in 1999—as a mail subscription service. If you remember those days during the stone age of the Internet, pokey dial-up connections were the norm, making video streaming virtually impossible. And pioneers who had actually ventured onto the web viewed the online and television universes as entirely separate entities.

In those early days, Netflix tried to sell out to Blockbuster for $50 million but couldn't cut a deal. So it was forced to innovate to survive. Luckily, Internet technology began to improve rapidly, making it possible for customers to stream programming through PCs or consoles like the Xbox. Now, of course, consumers pull programming directly through their web-enabled smart TVs or through devices like Apple TV or Roku.

As we all know, those video stores on every street corner closed, while Netflix just keeps growing and growing. Now besides offering existing TV shows and movies, it is producing original series of its own (including the ultrasuccessful *House of Cards* and new additions like *Grace and Frankie*), successfully competing with the cable giant HBO.

And Netflix did all of this using its core product—movies and TV programming—and tactically applying digital technology.

A New Model

Clearly, technology has changed dramatically since I wrote *Win One for the Shareholders* in 2008, and during that time, I have used this new technology in my turnarounds.

Accordingly, I have altered my original turnaround model and building blocks to the model that follows:

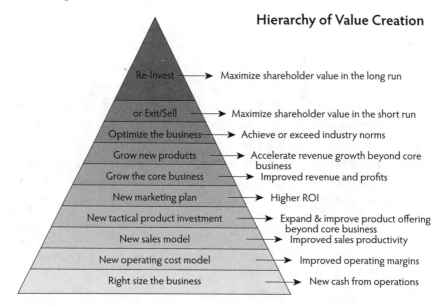

Hierarchy of Value Creation

Re-Invest → Maximize shareholder value in the long run

or Exit/Sell → Maximize shareholder value in the short run

Optimize the business → Achieve or exceed industry norms

Grow new products → Accelerate revenue growth beyond core business

Grow the core business → Improved revenue and profits

New marketing plan → Higher ROI

New tactical product investment → Expand & improve product offering beyond core business

New sales model → Improved sales productivity

New operating cost model → Improved operating margins

Right size the business → New cash from operations

Now it's time to develop a win/win strategy and employ the tactics that will allow you to implement my turnaround model. Just like in a game of chess, you will need a strategy to carry you from the beginning of your turnaround game to the winning conclusion. In the next chapter, I'll show you how to build the right battle plan.

Employ a Win/Win Strategy and Killer Tactics

STEP 9

A good plan, violently executed now, is better than a perfect plan executed next week. **General George Patton**

Strategy without tactics is the slowest route to victory . . . and every battle is won or lost before it's ever fought. **Unknown**

You know now that with my turnaround model in your back pocket, it's possible to turn a distressed business from an almost worthless enterprise into pure shareholder gold. Now I'll show you how to combine a strategy Sun Tzu would be proud of and killer tactics to win the war of execution or implementation.

Let's begin by crafting what I call a win/win strategy.

Building a Win/Win Strategy

This is how it always happens. I'm called in to do a turnaround because the business is failing. (Let me say it again: the business is *failing*.) And right from the start, management contends that its strategy is perfect; they can't understand why it is failing. As I noted in the introduction to Section II, a recent survey by the

"However beautiful the strategy, you should occasionally look at the result."

Turnaround Management Association showed that a majority of managers in failing businesses hang on to failed strategies. In fact, I have found that they hold tightly to the security blanket of those strategies right up to the point of the shareholder revolt that opens the door for me to help. The following saying puts the finger right on the problem: "However beautiful the strategy, you should occasionally look at the result." Strategies are about results, not perfection. To that point, strategies are a means to an end or specific result. They are not about perfect ideas that feel good and look good on paper.

There is no better example of a *perfect* strategy gone awry than Commodore Business Machines. While most people think that it was Apple that gave birth to the personal computer, it was actually Commodore. The company began life as a typewriter and watch repair company, then became a calculator manufacturer. Venturing into the burgeoning chip market, the company eventually developed the first personal computer, the Commodore PET, leading to the development of the Commodore 64, which broke all computer sales records.

Commodore was the first to sell home computers to the mass market through department stores, driving prices down and decimating most of the competition. Selling nearly twenty-two million units, the company took in nearly $681 million in 1983. Commodore's profits increased 85 percent that year. In fact, the computer maker's growth rate was nearly twice that of Apple and Tandy. In 1983, Commodore's global market share soared to 32 percent. Continuing the innovation, in 1983 Commodore brought out the SX-64, the first portable color computer, and the Plus/4 pioneered integrated software in ROM the following year.

Then came the age of Amiga. In 1985, Commodore introduced the world's first multimedia computer, the Amiga 1000. The Amiga was way ahead of its time. It actually had custom chips providing accelerated video in 4,096 colors, along with built-in outputs for TVs and VCRs—a prediction of the eventual merge with home entertainment systems. It was by far the most advanced system available for home use.

Unfortunately, the flashy new computer never made it big in the marketplace. For one thing, it was too ahead of its time—users were not yet able to appreciate the cool graphics and sound, viewing the computer as a mere game machine. And the company did little to support the product launch, failing to bolster it with marketing or consumer education. And that was just the beginning of the slide down the slippery slope.

In the beginning, it seemed that founder and president Jack Tramiel had his finger on the pulse of the industry. In fact, his aggressive strategy of vertical integration, massive production, and lower cost for consumers defined the standards of the industry. But even as Commodore hit the billion-dollar mark, it racked up piles of debt, which should have been proof that the company strategy was no longer working and a signal to shift gears.

Instead, things went from bad to worse. Tramiel resigned, and investor Irving Gould took the reins. Gould proved totally out of synch with industry trends, refusing to build PC-compatible hardware or software systems. Soon, users were turning to more compatible systems like IBM, and Commodore was becoming obsolete. The founding member of the home computer industry was completely derailed because it couldn't take an honest look at its strategy and see where it was going wrong.

Winning and Winning Some More

As the Commodore example demonstrates so beautifully, in a turnaround situation *strategies are about results and not ideas that sound good on paper.* Recognition of that truth through my years of work in failing businesses has led to the first independent element of my turnaround formula. I call it the creation of a win/win strategy

In a
turnaround
situation
*strategies are
about results
and not ideas
that sound
good on
paper.*

Regardless
of the turn of
events you
may face,
you need to
stick to your
resolution to
win, win, win.

The only
strategy that
works is one
that improves
the short-term
and long-term
results from
*the core thesis
or idea that
launched the
company.*

because it has two possible results. The first *win* is achieved by making sure your turnaround stabilizes the company for a potential sale, which is the most likely outcome. The second *win* is achieved by also planning for the fact that the company could make a second run at normal operating success if it chooses not to be sold after it has been turned around. The win/win approach of identifying both short- and long-term results to drive new shareholder value is the benchmark for any strategy that I ultimately deploy in a turnaround.

Let me point out that this same kind of thinking can be applied to an individual facing a personal or career failure. You should always be thinking about how to use the win/win strategy to come out a winner from any situation. This fits perfectly with your newfound goal to be a winner all the time, in any situation. Regardless of the turn of events you may face, you need to stick to your resolution to win, win, win.

And remember that a turnaround by nature—whether in business or personal life—does not involve the creation of a new concept. In turnarounds, the idea that originally drove creation of the business is already deeply engrained in all aspects of the business. So starting with a de novo idea as part of the turnaround strategy never works. Instead, the only strategy that works is one that improves the short-term and long-term results from *the core thesis or idea that launched the company.* On a personal level, as I pointed out earlier in the book, your turnaround involves using your innate talents and strengths to create new opportunities for success and wealth. Like a company with talented managers, you have within you the ability to manage your personal turnaround—you simply need to identify and fortify your talents.

Look at how Marvel, the comic book world's biggest player, went bankrupt in the mid-1990s but stayed with its core thesis and product ideas to turn the company around. Marvel's core products were Spider-Man, Captain America, and other superheroes. Marvel pivoted from comic books, ink, and paper to the movie screen and simply changed the medium of its original product ideas. Marvel did not try to futilely pivot into a new world with a new product.

When Peter Cuneo came on the scene as Marvel CEO in 1999, the company was just emerging from its bankruptcy nightmare and its stock price couldn't climb up over the one dollar mark. So the new leader resolved to make the company's eight thousand characters live up to their "super" reputations by extending their value across a number of media. He initiated a licensing model for movies, television, and consumer products; divested some loss-making businesses; reorganized the company around five operating units; and reduced operating costs. Ten years later, the company's stock stood at fifty-four dollars a share, and it sold out to Disney for $4.5 billion.

In a number of similar situations—including at Clairol and Black & Decker—Cuneo has proven a master at using a company's innate talents and assets to build a successful turnaround strategy.

Because Something Always Goes Wrong

From the very beginning of a turnaround process, it's critical to create a win/win strategy. Think about it: in every situation in life, there is always the chance that things will work out better than expected but also the accompanying possibility that something will go awry. You need to be prepared to turn each eventuality into a win. An old adage seems appropriate here: *hope for the best, but plan for the worst.*

So once a win/win strategy has been identified from the top down, it is very important to validate it from the bottom up. The best way to explain this is to walk you through a real-life turnaround situation that I managed for some very unhappy shareholders. The shareholders brought me into a company that was under the threat of a legal action against the directors and officers of the company. This company was in bad shape when I took over, and it was made worse by the bankers who froze the credit lines after I took over. This, of course, made my job doubly difficult.

I remember the sleepless nights thinking I had one small chance of success and no room for mistakes. I live by the motto that you are only as good as your last deal, and this one felt like the one that was going to bite me in the butt. I had one shot at getting a win/win strategy right, so I came up with the following plan:

- First, I needed to lessen my downside by quickly cutting expenses and gaining short-term credit from the bank so that I could fund restructuring costs and deleverage the balance sheet to create some breathing room and financial stability. Once this was accomplished, I had some cash to reinvest in sales and marketing to reverse the declining revenue line and get the company back to normalcy. It took us one full year to accomplish this, but then we were able to position the company for sale with a clean balance sheet, profitability, and some growth on the top line.
- Second, I needed to plan for my upside in the event that we could not find a buyer for the company or the board of directors decided it would not sell the company. I did this by having capital and bankers in place so we would have the leverage we needed to do a major acquisition.

In the end, we sold the company at a big profit and it lived happily ever after, at least as of the writing of this book.

Bottoms Up

As I said above, to be successful, you need to create your win/win strategy from the bottom up. Here's how you build that foundation:

First, identify and understand the immediate threat facing the company and the extent of the effort that it will take to nullify the threat. It only makes sense that you must properly identify and understand the real threat to the company before you can begin a corrective course of action. If you get this wrong, I can assure you that you will fail and run out of money and time to effect a turnaround.

Second, you need to understand the remaining strengths of the company and what assets you have at hand that can be deployed to execute the turnaround. Included in this calculation are the energy, commitment, willpower, and leadership of your team that can be applied to reverse the negative momentum in the business. Think of the rule of physics that states that the energy to stop an object must be equal to the force propelling the object forward (or in this case downward). There is no way to stop the downward momentum of the business unless the strengths and assets remaining in the company are equal to the task. On a personal level, that means identifying and effectively using your innate talents to stop a freefall into the abyss of failure.

Third, understand the real pivot points in the business that drive profitable sales and revenue. As they say in Silicon Valley, "feed those winners while you starve the losers," the areas of the business that do not drive sales and revenue. As Henry David Thoreau said, "It is not enough to be busy; so are the ants. The question is, what are we busy about?"

Finally, you need to be sure the financial model that you create prepares you for the worst-case scenario. It's not good enough to plan for the best- or medium-case scenarios. (We all know

As Henry David Thoreau said, "It is not enough to be busy; so are the ants. The question is, what are we busy about?"

what happens when you fail to plan for the worst; it inevitably happens!) The simplest way to identify your worst-case scenario is to extend the current sales, revenue, profit, and cash trend line for another year and superimpose your planned expense reductions and sales changes. If the model offers the financial stability you need—under even the worst circumstances—you have a good chance of stabilizing the situation long enough to execute a successful turnaround.

Chess, Not Checkers

One more element remains in crafting your win/win strategy after you have identified your specific financial goals, then covered the downside and upside cases from the top down and validated them from the bottom up. You need to understand that a turnaround, whether on a personal or business basis, involves a complicated and well-executed strategy, with moves planned from the very beginning of the turnaround game. Think chess rather than checkers; there's no benefit to diving in headfirst and jumping all over the board. Your game has to be played out in a careful and thoughtful way from the very beginning.

In fact, when I'm planning a turnaround strategy, I often set a chess table in front of me and identify all of the pieces on the board in order to visualize how the game should play out. As an avid chess admirer, it helps me to put all of the pieces in perspective once my win/win strategy is in place and validated to understand how the turnaround needs to be played out. I can't stress enough that the way you play the turnaround game is as important as how hard you play it. Mistakes are potential turnaround killers in this high-stakes game, and you must know your moves two or three steps in advance.

My chess board has the following players:

The turnaround executive is the chess master.
The shareholders are represented by the king (the one who loses in checkmate).

The queen is the board of directors whose goal is to protect the king.

The knights are the banks and other secured or unsecured lenders who need to protect the financial flanks and ensure solvency during the turnaround.

The rooks/castles are the key management and sales executives who must carry the offense and move the revenue line up.

The bishops are the day-to-day staff, specifically the middle managers who need to keep the train running.

The pawns are rightsized staff, projects, activities, businesses, vendors, and anything that will be sacrificed for the benefit of the king and the ultimate winning of the game.

This example of a chessboard always helps me understand and control my turnarounds as the game plays out and actions have to be taken to win.

Armed with a win/win strategy to protect you, you're now ready to learn how to use killer turnaround tactics.

Killer Tactics

It is the rigorous and creative application of killer tactics that brings true success in any turnaround—personal or business. Why use the term "killer tactics"? For one simple reason. If in the execution of a tactic some pain is not felt by both the giver and the receiver of the tactical action, the tactic is probably ineffective. As the saying goes, "no pain, no gain."

In every distressed company, management is busy executing meaningless tactics that are not

> It is the rigorous and creative application of killer tactics that brings true success in any turnaround— personal or business.

improving the performance of the company and are expending valuable resources and time. Why? As I demonstrated in Section I of this book, these managers are not mentally prepared to conquer their own fears of failure and win. Instead, they have grown too comfortable in their own delusions and are content to pretend to be dealing with the crisis at their gate. They have yet to find the courage to make the difficult moves that will save their company. As you will see, the tactics I use all have teeth in them; they cause the real pain that comes with real change and progress.

Before laying out those tactics, let me set the stage and explain how important tactics are to overall victory in distressed situations. No better example exists than the World War II naval Battle of Midway. The Japanese Navy had just decimated Pearl Harbor and a major part of the U.S. Pacific fleet in a surprise attack. The Imperial forces were planning a follow-up attack on the island of Midway that would have essentially eliminated the U.S. Navy's capabilities in the Pacific. This would have left the American West Coast undefended, paving the way for a Japanese invasion of the U.S. mainland. (If that had happened, you may have been reading this book in Japanese!)

As a starting point for a win/win strategy, Admiral Chester Nimitz first placed the two aircraft carriers that had survived the Pearl Harbor attack, the Enterprise and the Hornet, in position to defend against Japanese forces either waging an attack on Midway or invading the West Coast. Then the Navy achieved a seemingly impossible task by getting the aircraft carrier Yorktown back to sea in three weeks after it had been crippled in the Pearl Harbor attack. (To this day, it is viewed as one of the greatest accomplishments of World War II, and it gave the United States a much-needed element of surprise.)

But the really amazing and "violent" tactical move was to fearlessly attack the Japanese fleet instead of withdrawing and defending the three aircraft carriers. What a tactical risk! Can you imagine if the United States had lost those three carriers in the Battle of Midway? You get the point about executing point-of-the-spear tactics that have real teeth and potential pain in the heat of battle.

Make no mistake about it: when executing a turnaround, you are fighting a war. If it fails, it can be a career killer; destroy investment capital, jobs, and families; and permanently damage frail psyches. Therefore, the tactics I have developed are tough, no-nonsense, and potentially painful because the stakes are high and *failure is not an option.*

Tactic 1: Feed the Winners and Starve the Losers

Regardless of whether it's a sales representative or a specific business unit, if an entity is far from meeting its budget objective and required results, immediately cut off the blood flow. You need to deploy precious cash and capital being absorbed by that entity to one that is achieving results and meeting its budget. Of course, people vested in the entity will try to convince you to keep throwing good money after bad. Don't listen! You need to feed that cash and capital to your winners.

Tactic 2: Stop Selling "Bad Revenue" and Putting It into Your Factory

Salespeople in distressed companies are notorious for "selling against the house," as I like to say, by discounting and selling poor quality business to feather their sales goals and prop up the company's revenue line. This just complicates and increases the expense of your factory and business fulfillment process. If sales and corresponding revenue do not meet certain profitability requirements, they should not be allowed into the factory. I know the old argument about how even one dollar of bad sales or revenue covers a great deal of necessary overhead. I consider that a bogus argument. It's much more prudent to cut the overhead expense and stop perpetuating the problem!

Tactic 3: The First Fifteen to Twenty Cents of Every Sales Dollar Goes to the House (Shareholders)

To ensure that the company survives, it's critical to take funds right off the top of every sale to shore up company profitability. I like to tell the team that they are not working for a not-for-profit company. In fact, I like to position the company as a casino that never loses. In keeping with that vision, a minimum of fifteen cents of every dollar in sales should go to company profits first, with the remaining eighty-five cents used to run the business. Managers hate this pay-the-shareholders-first mentality because they've never faced the pressures of an entrepreneur and the reality of having to produce a real cash profit to pay the bills. Despite negative reactions, you should stick to the discipline of paying the house first. Otherwise, the company will not have the profitability and market position it needs to survive the turnaround.

Tactic 4: Fire the Bottom 5 Percent of Sales Personnel Each Year, Regardless of Results

In distressed companies, it's easy to discard normal "growth" sales goals and replace them with what I call "survival goals." All too often, sales forces in distressed companies abuse the desperate environment by negotiating goals that will never lead to growth. By nature, salespeople tend to just achieve their goal without over-achieving. I throw cold water on that idea by announcing I'll be firing the bottom 5 to 10 percent of producers, even if they have achieved their goals. The slackers usually quit at that point, so I can use their salary for producers who really want to work hard and exceed their sales goals.

Tactic 5: Be the Low-Cost and High-Quality Provider in Your Industry Now

Stop deluding yourself that your brand and products are still winners and that the world will one day come back to its senses and start buying your products again. If you are failing, it's because you have fallen behind the competitive curve for numerous reasons, and you need to give your target audiences a reason to buy from you again. So make them an offer they can't refuse with new lower-cost offerings. While you may not be bringing in as much revenue per sale, you are finally bringing a flow of resources back into the business and generating new profit for shareholders. Keep in mind that you need to roll out these new lower-cost offerings while maintaining high-quality standards, and the world will start to once again beat a path to your door.

Tactic 6: Simplify, Simplify, Simplify

Streamline every aspect of the business from the point of sale to the mail room, eliminating all unnecessary functions and expenses. In every company I have touched, a minimum of 20 percent of expenses and activities can be eliminated without any negative impact on the business or its customers. In one turnaround, we eliminated $100 million of expenses and activities, and the company actually operated more efficiently. The company was a $300 million company, so one-third of all of its expenses were removed without a hitch or stumble. So don't listen to people who swear this kind of reduction will destroy the company. The process actually makes the company lighter—less bogged down by nonproductive activities—and better able to respond to changes and demands in the marketplace.

Tactic 7: Share the Wealth

While the first six tactics are pain points, the seventh is the reward. You need your leadership team and key employees behind you through the tough territory ahead, so it's important to guarantee them a big payday at the end of the successful turnaround. So use all your negotiating skills to convince the board of directors and shareholders that the team should be properly incentivized. Team members will be more likely to push through the turnaround—whatever it takes—if they know that their house will be paid off, children's college years funded, or other life dreams achieved. Don't be a pig; pay the team and share the wealth.

The Finishing Touch: Finding the Right Leader to Implement Your Win/Win Strategy and Killer Tactics

> *A leader is one who knows the way, goes the way, and shows the way.* **John C. Maxwell, author of *The 21 Irrefutable Laws of Leadership***

It's easy to make the mistake of thinking that because you run or manage a business, you can be the commanding general through a

You might say
that the right
turnaround
leader is like
a Spartan
warrior who
is prepared
to be "carried
out on his
shield"

turnaround. After all, you've built the business from scratch and been at the helm for years, through all phases and growth. Who could be better suited to take the company through this harrowing period?

You may think that's a rhetorical question—it's not! There is someone better suited to take the reins through the war you're about to wage. The right leader for a distressed company facing a turnaround is a different breed from the right person to maintain a business or help it function in a stable environment. It's the difference between being a general sitting behind a desk in Washington, DC, in peacetime and the general in the forward command center during a war. The wartime general faces constant risk and could easily go down with his troops, while the peacetime general functions in a business-as-usual bubble.

In turnarounds—as in war—there is no place to hide. It takes a uniquely fearless leader to assume that much responsibility and risk, both personally and professionally. You might say that the right turnaround leader is like a Spartan warrior who is prepared to be "carried out on his shield" rather than accept defeat. I believe that kind of iron will is exceedingly rare. While many businesspeople claim to welcome the challenge of a turnaround, most come unglued the minute the going gets really rough. When that happens, the whole turnaround—which must be precisely planned and executed—is at risk.

The *Really* Right Stuff

Through my years of working through turnarounds, I have identified what I consider to be the key characteristics that a leader needs to wage the turnaround war.

First and foremost, the leader must be calm and firm in a crisis, and as the crisis intensifies, he or she must become calmer and more steadfast. The leader's heart rate needs to go down in a crisis, not up. Can you imagine what might have happened if President Kennedy hadn't been calm and steadfast in the Cuban Missile Crisis? What if he had panicked or overreacted by bombing the Russian missile silos inside Cuba? I have no doubt that World War III would have started. So when you look for that quality of calm in a leader for a turnaround or crisis, think about Kennedy.

The second most important quality is the ability, as the Marines say, to adapt and overcome adversity. I don't care how well you plan; things are going to go wrong. No one can account for all of the variables in a crisis. In fact, if you can claim an average of about 75 percent accuracy with strategy, implementation planning, and tactics, you are doing well. That means you'll have to adapt and change your strategy about 25 percent of the time. You need a leader who can roll with the punches and adapt when it becomes necessary.

The perfect example of just such a leader is Bill Belichick, coach of the New England Patriots. Every week during the NFL season, he and his team wage war on a constantly changing playing field. No matter how carefully the coach and his star quarterback Tom Brady construct strategy, they are sure to be surprised by variables like players' injuries, mistakes, and surprises from the other team.

But Belichick is never derailed by problems that invariably arise during a game; he is the master of halftime adjustments, adapting and overcoming adversity as it comes. He has cultivated the ability to creatively and flexibly adjust his players and plans, improvise, and overcome the challenge. (By the way, I have to take a cheap shot at my home team, the New York Giants, who made a huge mistake in not offering Belichick the head coach job when it had the chance back in the 1980s. It failed to see his incredible ability for performing under pressure and have paid the price for that mistake ever since! Clearly, the Giants' leadership didn't know what it didn't know.)

The third major characteristic to seek in a crisis leader is the ability to identify, focus, and motivate good talent from outside

and within the organization. As the famous UCLA basketball coach John Wooden said, "Whatever you do in life, surround yourself with smart people who will challenge you and you will be successful." Or as Jack Welch, one of the most respected CEOs in U.S. history said, "The team with the best players wins. . . . My main job was developing talent. I was a gardener providing water and other nourishment to our top 750 people. Of course, I had to pull out some weeds, too."

Now let's move on to the final step in your move toward success and wealth and see how I have learned to invest in myself to build significant wealth.

STEP 10 | How I Learned to Invest in Myself and Create Wealth

I will tell you how to become rich. Close the door. Be fearful when others are greedy. Be greedy when others are fearful.
Warren Buffett

The stock market is filled with individuals who know the price of everything and the value of nothing. **Philip Fisher**

By now you should have caught on to the central notion of this book: failure, once it's *harnessed*, can be a great opportunity for success and wealth. Nowhere is that clearer than in the turnaround world, where savvy investors and operators can make big profits if they know the secret formula for investing in TUCs.

No More Fear

Now that you've learned how to view failure as a gift, understand how to marshal your resources to tame it, and have my proven turnaround model in your back pocket, I want to share with you my Ten Golden Rules of Investing in Turnarounds. I caution that my ten golden rules are not investment advice or

> I believe investing in turnarounds is one of the *best* opportunities to create new wealth.

recommendations for you to use as an amateur or unqualified investor. These rules constitute a system that has worked for me over the years, and I am sharing them with you so that you can form your own opinions on how to invest in yourself when the opportunity surfaces. As the old Latin saying goes, caveat emptor—or let the buyer (or in this case, investor) beware.

Guidelines and Protection

Over the twenty-five years of my turnaround career, I've developed these rules as a discipline to carry me through the arduous process of the turnaround. But they have also proven to be invaluable tools in my investment life. By doing the necessary research and following these rules to the letter, I entered an entirely new world of opportunity. In fact, in today's investment world, I believe investing in turnarounds is one of the *best* opportunities to create new wealth. This is the ultimate proof of the idea presented at the outset of this book. Failure offers the only opportunity for real growth, change, and success.

Steer Clear of Bankruptcies

But let's be clear about one thing: wise investing does not involve bankruptcies. Bankruptcy is the most extreme level of distress, and it's a game for lawyers, bankers, and specialists who know how to work the legal system and the banking laws. When a company can no longer pay its bills and needs to protect itself through bankruptcy laws, underlying equity of the company is essentially worthless. This creates a graveyard for investors who are not legal and financial engineering experts. So don't be tempted to participate in a private offering or any opportunity to buy the equity in a bankrupt or near bankrupt company! This is a horrible environment for doing a business turnaround or investing as an individual or small investment organization.

The perfect example of this is the Lehman Brothers fiasco back in 2007 and 2008. Despite a raft of bad investments and collapsing stock price, everyone from the chairman of Lehman to the U.S. secretary of the Treasury declared that the company was solvent. Thousands of investors were seduced by the bargain-basement stock price, convinced they'd make a killing when the company rebounded.

That rebound never happened. Instead, the company went begging for a bailout that never came when Uncle Sam decided it was too big for the government's appetite. In a New York minute, Lehman's equity was wiped out, and the company disappeared from the corporate landscape. Scores of amateur investors lost their shirts, while expert bankruptcy investors who had seen the debacle coming lined their pockets.

Incidentally, Lehman is by far the biggest bankruptcy in American corporate history, followed by WorldCom and Enron. Just look at the amount of equity lost in these failures!

1. Lehman Brothers: $639 billion

2. WorldCom: $103 billion

3. Enron: $63 billion

Focusing on TUCs

Rather than bankruptcies, I focus on troubled and underperforming public companies that have been experiencing sustained financial and operating performance failures for at least a year. (It takes one full year—or four reporting quarters—for the true nature of the problem to surface in a failing public company.) But while these companies show signs of sustained failure, they are not hopeless causes. If they take the appropriate corrective actions at the delicate "point of inflection" or "pivot point," they can reverse their negative momentum and pivot upward. And this is the key to my investment strategy: when the stock moves upward, new wealth—turnaround gold—is created for investors.

Greenfield Online is a perfect example of a company that was clearly failing. Over about a year, its stock price collapsed from more than twenty dollars per share to less than five dollars. But there were clear signs the company was basically strong; it was never a bankruptcy candidate and had plenty of cash on the balance sheet. Savvy investors knew that shareholder value could be recaptured if the right corrective actions were taken under the direction of an experienced turnaround expert. And because Greenfield was a public company, they could see the corrective actions play out in the public domain and buy and sell accordingly.

Investors' faith was amply rewarded when my team and I fixed the problems at Greenfield in less than two years and sold to Microsoft for $17.50 a share. This is a perfect example of how to make money and get rich by fixing failure and investing accordingly.

Of course, the trick to success using this investment strategy is learning how to pick winners like Greenfield among hundreds of troubled and failing public companies. As any experienced investor will tell you, you do that by first employing big portions of native instinct and old-fashioned common sense. As Benjamin Graham wrote in his famous 1949 book, *The Intelligent Investor*, "Intelligent investment is more a matter of mental approach than it is of technique."

Once I fired up my instinct and common sense, I realized I needed a technique for putting them to work. In the world of turnaround investing, the technique that rewarded my prospecting was the discipline of my Ten Golden Rules.

Let's take a look at each of these rules, along with examples of how they play out in real life.

Golden Rule 1: Wait for the "Capitulation Event" in the Failing Company and Its Stock Price before Considering an Investment

I never allow myself to be tempted to buy as the failing company's stock begins its decline. In these early stages, existing investors are knee-deep in denial, convinced the company is "doing just fine" despite glaring signs of failure. (Remember when earlier in the book I described the denial and delusion syndrome that strikes managers and directors? Investors get stuck in the same trap.) The full impact of impending failure isn't reflected in the stock price until investors finally face reality and begin to abandon ship.

For a variety of reasons—including volume of trading, concentration of positions, influence of a few key shareholders, and boards of directors that are slow to react—it can take a year for the failure to lead to a capitulation event. This event ranges from the bank shutting down the company's line of credit, to one of the stock exchanges threatening to delist the company, to lawsuits being filed. When one of these events happens, existing investors can no longer ignore reality, and the stock sinks to its true value. (I can assure you that it always does find the true valuation because markets tend to do that; it just takes longer with a failing company.)

A perfect example of this phenomenon is Sears Holdings Corporation, which has retreated from its high of $150 dollars per share in 2007 to around $7 today. See the following sidebar for a look at the company's travails.

Sears Stock Chart

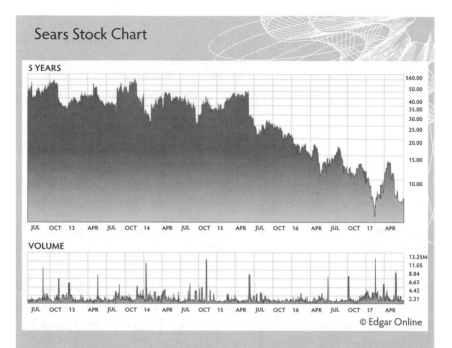

5 YEARS

© Edgar Online

Sears has been a distressed public company for many years. The king of retail for more than a century, the company never successfully made the transition from outdated brick-and-mortar operations to today's gold standard, online retailing. And Sears has consistently struggled with issues around its acquisition of discount retailer Kmart.

If years ago you had bought into Sears, thinking you could gauge when its stock had hit bottom, you would have racked up huge losses as the stock continued to decline. Why? There has never been a defining *capitulation event* to build a solid floor under the stock price. Instead, the company has simply tumbled ever closer to bankruptcy, with nothing definitive to break its fall. Although the word *bankruptcy* seems to be attaching itself to Sears as I write this book and a capitulation event could be in the works, it could also be something worse. This is a sad state of affairs for an American icon.

Road Signs a Capitulation Is Approaching
So what are the specific signs that a true capitulation has occurred and the stock is at or near its bottom? A capitulation event is usually preceded by one or more of these events:

1. The bank(s) cancels, suspends, or does not renew working capital lines of credit.

2. The cash on hand to run the business without the line of credit falls to nine months or less of operating cash.

3. An "ongoing concern" opinion is given by the auditors.

4. The CFO resigns or is fired.

5. A quarterly earnings report forecasts a sharp drop in sales and revenue after several previous earnings reports (usually four) fell below prior year performance.

6. A large shareholder acts in a way that results in the termination of the CEO and hiring of a true turnaround expert. In some cases, board members resign or are replaced as well.

7. There is a class action or government lawsuit, claiming a dereliction of fiduciary duties by the company and its executives and the board of directors.

8. The company has too much long-term debt and the potential for default.

Any one or a combination of these eight signs—in a company experiencing downward trajectory in its performance and stock price for one year or more—signals an imminent capitulation in the stock price.

I have learned that, as an investor, I need to be patient and wait for the moment of capitulation in the stock price to give me the

I have learned
that, as an
investor, I
need to be
patient and
wait for the
moment of
capitulation
in the stock
price to give
me the lowest
possible price.

lowest possible price. As an example of how that works, I have turned down numerous opportunities to do turnarounds as CEO or a consultant because the price of the stock had not capitulated. Because I am paid largely in stock or options, I can't determine what my compensation will be when the turnaround is successful if I can't find the floor in the stock price.

I always make sure my risk is on the upside and not the downside value of the stock price.

Golden Rule 2: Identify the Potential for an Extraordinary Rate of Return on Your Investment Relative to the Associated Risk

An extraordinary return would be 25 to 33 percent annually during the term of an investment. Capital is precious and time is money, so I don't waste time on investments that are not financial game changers, especially when there is a meaningful risk of losing money.

I like to target a 200 to 300 percent total return on my investment in a failing public company over a two-year period. In fact, my historical rates of return on my turnarounds are a 270 percent gross multiple, with a 38 percent internal rate of return. Granted, I am in control of my own destiny because I am responsible for fixing the problems and turning around the company. But if I did not insist on taking deals where the capitulation event in the stock price had occurred or was close to occurring, I would have had a much higher cost base and my returns on investment would have been drastically reduced.

The underlying point is that even in the best turnarounds, there is only so much room for improvement, and the investor does not have an infinite upside. A good example of this point is one of my more recent deals where I took on the turnaround as CEO and the stock had—for the most part—capitulated to around seventy-five cents per share. (It did actually sink lower, but I came pretty close to calling the bottom before I took the assignment.)

Over sixteen months, my team and I fixed most of the problems in the company and stabilized an organization that would otherwise have drifted into bankruptcy. At that point, a larger competitor was interested in purchasing the newly viable company, creating a 185 percent return for investors and me. While this was less than the return I usually target, it had become clear that restoring viability was all we could do to improve the badly damaged company; there was no way to remake it into a growth company where the stock price would have gone much higher on sale.

Because my investors and I were realistic about how high the company and its stock were likely to climb, we took advantage of the opportunity in front of us. And because we had waited for the capitulation event to take on the turnaround, we had the lowest possible cost basis for the investment. The old strategy of "buy low and sell high" is what investing in failure and turnarounds is all about. I don't overanalyze the car wreck. I salvage and fix what I can and sell it to the highest bidder; that's the game!

An important note is that I don't allow myself to feel guilty about seeking returns of 200 to 300 percent; it is not my fault that the distressed company hit the skids. I think of it this way: I've worked hard to conquer the fear of failure and put my hard-earned capital to work in a failing company. I deserve to be rewarded. In fact, I believe

> The old strategy of "buy low and sell high" is what investing in failure and turnarounds is all about. I don't overanalyze the car wreck. I salvage and fix what I can and sell it to the highest bidder; that's the game!

I believe
turnaround
investing is
one of the
few remaining
areas of
rugged
individualism
left in today's
modern
investment
world.

I deserve to congratulate myself for taking the road less traveled by investing in a failing company. I believe turnaround investing is one of the few remaining areas of rugged individualism left in today's modern investment world. The essence of my philosophy to make your own fate is captured in the quote often attributed to Ralph Waldo Emerson: "To be yourself in a world that is constantly trying to make you something else is the greatest accomplishment."

I Don't Expect These Rates of Return Anywhere Else
Here's why turnaround investing is compelling for individuals seeking higher returns. Global markets have become incredibly efficient, pricing to perfection and making it next to impossible for active investment managers to beat the overall indexes or market averages.

In fact, a semiannual report produced by S&P Global in the September 2016 issue of *The Financial Times* reported that nine out of ten U.S. equity funds run by active managers or stock pickers failed to beat the market averages over the past year. This only makes sense because all managers and traders in today's connected global marketplace have the same public information and advanced tools. So every manager or trader out there is seeing the same opportunities as you in the traditional market.

In today's mainstream market, the only time investors can create value is by timing buying and selling cycles just right—selling just as a selling cycle begins or buying as a buying cycle begins. For example, one buying cycle began when, in 2008, the Federal Reserve reduced interest rates to zero to counteract the fiscal crisis that began the previous year. On the flip side, experts believe the selling cycle could be around the corner as the recovery goes into its ninth year. Investors have to be constantly tuned in to the market and ready to turn on a dime to make money in the current environment.

Despite its potential, turnaround investing is highly inefficient, volatile, and risky. But remember, it is exactly that volatility and risk that leads to extraordinary returns. In fact, I believe that in the world of the twenty-first century, with its universal access to information and education, the willingness to take risks and embrace and conquer failure are the only ways to pull away from the pack and create truly extraordinary returns on investments.

I, for one, have always followed my own path. I think I come by that self-reliance naturally, having descended from immigrants who came to this country determined to make their own way and provide for future generations. I learned from my father and grandfather that the only way to truly succeed is to carve out your own path. So I've made it my goal to find the "streets paved with gold" my ancestors sought when they got off the boat from Italy, and it's clear to me that I'll never do that by investing in the S&P 500.

Golden Rule 3: CYA (Cover Your Assets) and Make Sure Your Investment Downside Is Covered

Next, I compare the price of the stock at the time of capitulation with the cash value per share of the stock. If the gap between the two valuations is too large, that means the stock price is still too high. In that case, I wait and do nothing until the gap closes and my downside risk is tolerable.

My approach is to identify what I think is the capitulation price per share and then use the cash value per share price to identify the lowest price the stock will reach. If the capitulation price per share is more than 50 percent higher than the cash value per share, I wait until the gap closes before accepting the assignment and investing in the company. I have learned the hard way that you can never go wrong if you follow the guidance, *when in doubt, do nothing*! (By the way, through a lifetime of helping people solve problems, I have learned that this is a good rule to follow in every area of life.)

So here is how I calculate the cash value per share price:

1. What is the available cash on hand today and for the next twelve months to operate the company while the turnaround is in progress? (This includes cash in the bank and liquid investments, plus twelve months of receivables less payments due to banks, payroll, and 50 percent of forecasted current liabilities for the twelve month period. I use only 50 percent because I make loyal vendors who have lived off the company for years creditors until the company is out of the woods.)

2. I add a 15 percent reduction of annual operating costs that come out of the turnaround's immediate rightsizing of the company.

3. I then subtract approximately 25 percent of those same operating cost reductions to pay for severance and other restructuring charges associated with the rightsizing.

4. I then add back 75 percent of all current cash capital expenditures, which I usually suspend for the first twelve months of the turnaround. Any cash capital expenditures (Cap X) during that period are focused on maintenance-only activities.

5. I then add a conservative amount of cash that I can assign to small asset sales of noncore assets, including one-off businesses that do not fit the strategy of returning the company to its core competency. I sell these assets quickly, and I am not afraid to give a buyer a bargain to create additional cash for the turnaround and downside liquidity protection.

6. Finally, I subtract 5 percent of the net forecasted revenue for the year (net revenue is revenue after cost of goods

sold) to account for sales and revenue slippage, which is an automatic in failing companies; they invariably miss their sales targets.

To make the formula more concrete, I have created the following hypothetical example.

Failing Company Alpha has $100 million forecasted revenue for the next twelve months, down from $105 million the previous year and $115 million the year before. The company is losing 10 percent on its bottom line and has an operating income loss of $10 million, which is a $10 million cash loss for all practical purposes. The bank is about to freeze Alpha's credit line, and Alpha owes the bank $7 million, of which $3 million in principal and interest payments are due over the next twelve months. Alpha has twenty million publically traded shares outstanding and its stock has collapsed from a high of $15 on its initial public offering (IPO) five years ago to what appears to be a "capitulation" stock price of $1 today after the bank announced it was suspending the credit line and NASDAQ said it was considering a delisting. What is the net operating cash value of this company that underlies a turnaround and creates the floor for building new shareholder value from a turnaround?

Cash on hand calculation = $6 million

Add cash savings from rightsizing operations = $15 million

Subtract cash restructuring expenses = $4 million

Add 75 percent reduction of cash savings from Cap X suspension = $5 million

Add cash from noncore assets sales = $5 million

Subtract cash impact of 5 percent revenue miss = ($5 million)

Total = $22 million in available cash divided by 20 million shares = $1.10 per share in cash

This one is a no-brainer because the capitulation price of the stock of $1 and the cash value per share of $1.10 align to create a reasonably true picture of what my downside is in the stock price once I accept the turnaround and make an investment. I would jump in here and buy stock, knowing that if I could fix the company I would have little or no downside and only upside from the value I create.

Golden Rule 4: Don't Make the Investment If You Don't Trust the Leadership of the Failing Company and Their Ability to Fix the Problems

Now that I know the price at which to buy into the failing company, I need to be sure the people in charge of the company and turnaround will safeguard my investment. So I ask myself, "Who am I betting on to deliver the upside and return on my investment?"

1. First, I ensure there is a proven leader with a track record of success in fixing failure—and ideally doing turnarounds—running the company. Fixing corporate failure requires a special skill set honed through years of learning to win regardless of the level of difficulty. If someone with that unique makeup is at the helm, the odds of success go up 100 percent. Do we need to look any further than quarterback Tom Brady, a five-time Super Bowl winner, or Jamie Dimon, chairman and CEO of JP Morgan, for examples of leaders determined to win at all costs? I need to see exactly that kind of superhuman determination in my potential investment. Without it, leadership will cave under the weight of adversity, the turnaround will fail, and I'll be throwing my money into the abyss of failure.

2. I determine if there are meaningful numbers of institutions or individuals with substantial holdings and equity as members of the board of directors or influencing the board of directors. This means the board

has skin in the game and will push to see that the problems are fixed. Generally speaking, it's critical to have the board's support behind fixing problems and possibly selling the company.

3. I find out if senior creditors, including the bank and preferred shareholders, are part of the team supporting the course correction or part of the problem. I also need to know if there is so much debt on the books that it will be impossible to make the company solvent.

4. Finally, I determine the condition of the management team, key sales leadership, and the intellectual capital in the company. Has senior management abandoned ship, or are they onboard and ready to go back to work? Also, are they part of an overall "can do" culture that wants to be successful, or are they just along for the ride until the music stops?

Golden Rule 5: Don't Make the Investment If You Don't Know What Caused the Company to Fail and Whether That Failure Can Be Fixed

After twenty-plus years of deals involving failing companies, I have found that our fear of failure as a society has caused us to overanalyze and complicate it. My work has taught me that there are three basic reasons for business failure:

1. Self-inflicted wounds by a board of directors, the CEO, and management team. In short, they "didn't know what

I have found that our fear of failure as a society has caused us to overanalyze and complicate it.

they didn't know" about running the company and made serious mental and execution errors in systemic areas like capital investment, merger and acquisition activity, leverage and debt, new product development, and staffing the executive team. Nothing creates failure in business—or life—like incompetence, and in my opinion, this is the number one reason companies fail.

2. The board and/or management has failed to respond appropriately to external factors. These can be factors that have either negatively impacted or provided an opportunity to improve the business. Often companies become so comfortable in their own skins that they don't feel the need to respond to change for a variety of bad reasons, ranging from laziness and complacency to stupidity. Do we need to look any further than Blockbuster and its nationwide chain of video stores missing the on-demand movie phenomenon driven by technological change? As I said in the last chapter, Netflix did not miss it!

3. Time has passed the company by and the megatrends of the new world have made the company and its business irrelevant and incapable of sustaining itself. A current example of this phenomenon is Bebe, the clothing retailer that just announced it is closing almost all of its two hundred nationwide retail stores. Bebe's survival issue, along with many other brick-and-mortar retailers, is the new megatrend of Amazon and online shopping, which now accounts for more than 50 percent of all nationwide sales. This trend is a dinosaur killer; it is the equivalent of a mass extinction event of a business species, and there is no escape for many of the players.

Golden Rule 6: Look for Intangibles or Hidden Assets That Make the Decision to Invest Less Risky

The following are examples of these intangibles:

1. Proven leadership and a good management team incentivized to work hard for two years and fix the problems of the company

2. A supportive board of directors and lead investors willing to let the CEO and management team "break some glass" and fix the problem, even if it means more downside to the stock price

3. A brand that provides an intangible underpinning to the business and clients' desire to continue working with the business through hard times

4. A viable product portfolio and technology platform that does not require massive capital expenditures to upgrade

5. A balance sheet that does not have to be restructured to provide a glide path for fixing the company

6. A culture among the employees that emphasizes saving the company

Golden Rule 7: Identify the Pivot Points and Benchmarks for Success

If I can identify those pivot points, do I have sufficient access to information, and is the company transparent enough to allow me to monitor those pivot points and the progress of the turn-around? Being able to monitor these pivot points allows me to bail from the investment if stated results are not being achieved or potentially double down on my investment if things are going better than planned. The key pivot points that I try to monitor with some precision are the progress of stated initiatives involving cost, sales, cash, and technology.

An example would be gaining a detailed understanding of how a bloated cost structure is being reduced. Is it coming from low-hanging fruit like cutting variable expense, or is the company unwinding complex and fixed general and administrative overhead expense? I want to know not only how much expense is being reduced but also exactly where it is coming from and how it is being eliminated too.

Golden Rule 8: Watch for Signs in the Stock Price

Becoming a growth company again changes the valuation of the company and upside stock price dramatically. There are particular actions and behaviors to watch to determine if and how much the top line of the company can grow during the turnaround. Two simple indicators give me a pretty good idea if a company in a turnaround will be able to grow its top line again or will simply struggle to salvage some value in the company by cutting expenses.

The first indicator is the productivity of the sales force and sales effort. Are individual salespeople and business units exceeding previous quarter sales results or not? I am not fooled by budgets and statements from the company that budget targets are being achieved. Either the company is growing relative to previous year results or it is not.

The second indicator is the measurement of the growth or lack thereof from announced new products or ventures designed to provide entry into new markets. This is the "new grass growing" example, where these products and ventures are like new green shoots; if they grow, the business thrives, and if they don't, it lingers and falls back to the world of distress.

Golden Rule 9: When Cash Is on the Table, Take It and Run

There is an old Wall Street saying made famous by TV commentator and analyst Jim Kramer: "Bulls make money, bears make money, and pigs get slaughtered." The point here is that when I have a healthy profit on the table, I take the cash and exit, either by selling in the legal open market windows or by waiting for the sale of the company and earning the 20 percent (or more) stock price premium that usually accompanies a sale. While I may be leaving some upside profit on the table, it comes with a lot of risk.

Investors in mobile phone company Blackberry have learned that lesson over the last ten years. While I believe the company has a great product and—believe it or not—I still use a Blackberry, it hasn't been able to keep pace with its prime competitor, the iPhone.

In its heyday in 2008, Blackberry stock rose to a high of $138, then collapsed with the rest of the world and went to $40 in 2009, when it began to run into competition from the iPhone and its clones. However, it did manage to recover during a mini-turnaround to $73 per share. The smart money got out in the rebound, but the pigs stayed in, hoping for the glory days of $138 to return. Today, Blackberry's stock is selling for $9 a share, and in my opinion, it is holding on for dear life, waiting for someone like Microsoft to buy them and connect them to their business user's platform. The moral is to take the cash when it is on the table.

Golden Rule 10: Work Hard to Keep Your Ego in Check

When I sell my stock at a handsome profit and am a little richer, I thank my lucky stars that everything went as planned, because the next deal or investment could be the one that bites me in the butt and could be my last! In the final chapter, let me pass on some closing thoughts about America, the journey you've completed, and the one that continues—a life free of the fear of failure and full of success.

Closing Thoughts

From Last to First

In Matthew 20:16, Jesus tells his disciples that "the last shall be first and the first shall be last." There are many interpretations and applications of this message, but the one that inspires me the most and that I have applied in my life is a message of *hope*. Whether you are an individual struggling with life and poverty or you are the leader of your business and it is failing, you deserve the gift of hope. I hope that is the gift I have given you in the pages of this book.

Once you have embraced the gift of hope, you need to have faith. As I hope I've proven in the pages you've just read, it's deeply embedded faith in yourself that eventually illuminates the path to your own turnaround and triumph over seemingly insurmountable challenges.

I have always been moved by the story of the Miracle of Dunkirk. In May 1940, in the early stages of World War II, the British and French armies had been badly defeated by the Germans in the Battle of France. The remains of the entire British army and major parts of the French and Belgian armies, estimated at more than 350,000 men, were trapped at the Port of Dunkirk, with the ocean at their backs and no escape from the advancing German army. The Germans were poised to slaughter the Allied forces on the beach and possibly deal a knockout blow, forcing surrender.

Led by Winston Churchill, the British launched a frantic rescue mission, hoping they could save a portion of their army. This would still have constituted a disaster, but perhaps enough forces would have remained to defend the homeland from the German invasion of England that was sure to come on the heels of the German victory in France. Then in what some have seen as a moment of divine intervention, an idea surfaced to put out a call to the civilian population and ask anyone with a boat on either side of the English Channel to head to Dunkirk and save as many soldiers as possible. Over a miraculous ten days from May 26 to June 4, these fishing boats, pleasure boats, yachts, and row boats—under aerial bombardment from the Germans—saved almost 340,000 men from the beaches of Dunkirk. The British army lived to fight another day and defeat the Germans, with a little help from their American cousins.

The more I read about events like Dunkirk, the more I appreciate the power of hope, faith, and hard work—when married to a creative strategy and plan—to produce an unimagined path out of dire and distressful circumstances. It has led me to the strong belief that almost any problem in life can be overcome.

For 250 years, there has been no better home for the trio of faith, hope, and hard work than America. As you've seen in this book, the stories abound of Americans who have defeated failure, picked themselves up by their bootstraps, and gone on to journey from the bottom to the top of society. In fact, I believe that American society is unique in its unfettered support of the journey from last to first. It is our culture of free will and free enterprise that gives everyone a real chance at success. This is the story and secret formula of every immigrant group that has ever come to America.

If America is to remain the hope of its current and future citizens, I believe it is critical to preserve this model of hope, faith, and hard work. While I understand the drive in every society to protect those least fortunate and offer more free services, I fear that America could go the way of bankrupt and failing societies around the world who have failed to promote and protect individual initiative and free enterprise. In fact, I believe that the unabated global trend toward big government or socialism is leading us down a path of unmanageable debt and destruction of this American dream where the last can become first.

These words from poet Carl Sandburg may be the best expression of my concerns for the future of America: "When a nation goes down, or a society perishes, one condition may always be found; they forgot where they came from. They lost sight of what had brought them along."

As a final note, as long as America embraces free enterprise and protects and promotes individual initiative, anyone born on the bottom of the American social ladder can go from last to first, as I have done in my life. I have embraced this dream both personally and intellectually, and it is my secret to success. As I hope I have made clear on the pages of this book, it takes plenty of hard work and dedication to make the turnaround miracle happen. But if you are willing to put together the trio of faith, hope, and hard work, you will be rewarded with the sense of peace and personal security that make life worthwhile.

That is my gift to you in this book. God bless!

"When a nation goes down, or a society perishes, one condition may always be found; they forgot where they came from. They lost sight of what had brought them along."

—Carl Sandburg

Index

poverty, 23, 28, 31, 33
predestined purpose, 25
price of success, 64–65
printing business, 7
private equity firms, 48
private offerings, 105
problem-solving, 23–24
production, massive, 89
productivity, 120
product life cycles, 83–85
product portfolios, 119
profitability, 97–98
prophecy, self-fulfilling, 27
Psychology Today, 2–3
public companies, 106
public service, 46
purpose, 19–36, 51

quality standards, 98
Queens College, 35
Quinctilius Varus, 43–44

randomness, 25
rates of return, 110–13
rationalizing, 51
Raymond, Lee, 75
Reagan, Ronald, 5, 15, 28–32, 48, 82
reality, staying rooted in, 50–51
recovery, path of, xi–xii
re-investing, 86
relationships, personal, 46–47
rendezvous with destiny, 26, 32
reorganization, 91
repeatability, 64–66
responsibility, xv–xvi, 5–9, 38
restructuring, 92, 114–15
results, 88, 89–90
retail, 108, 118
revenue
    bad, 97
    net, 114–15
revolts, shareholder, 88
rewards, managing, 51
rightsizing, 86, 114–15
risk, 50–51, 82, 113

Ritholtz, Barry, 42
Rockne, Knute, 31
Rocky Balboa, xi–xii
Rodriguez, Alex, 76
Roku, 85
Roman Empire, 43–44, 63
Roosevelt, Franklin D., 46, 63, 65
Rovio Entertainment, 56
rugged individualism, 112
Russell, Jamarcus, 76

sacrifices, 95
safety, 62
sales
    of companies, 86, 90–92, 111, 121
    goals, 98
    models, 86
    of noncore assets, 114–15
salespeople, 95, 97–98, 117, 120
Sandburg, Carl, 125
Sanders, Bernie, 69
San Diego Chargers, 76
S&P Global, 112
Sasson, Steve, 44
Sears Holding Corporation, 107–8
Secaucus, New Jersey, 29
self-actualization, 62
self-determination, 8
self-discovery, xiii
self-empowerment, 81
self-examination, 23
self-fulfilling prophecy, 27
self-inflicted wounds, 117–18
self-reliance, xv, 6–9
selling against the house, 97
selling cycles, 112–13
sequence of actions, 80
serial winners, 64–65
severance packages, 75–76, 114–15
shareholders, 88, 94, 97–98, 109, 119
shock and awe, 46
shock therapy, 39
shortcomings, admitting, 38
short-term results, 90
Shulman, Morton, 48

validation of strategies, 91
value creation hierarchy, 86
variables, accounting for, 101
vertical integration, 89
viability, restoring, 111
video streaming, 85
Vietnam War, 46
vision, 57, 69
volatility, 113

Walt Disney Company. *See* Disney
war, 33, 97, 100
Washington, Booker T., 8–9
wealth
    concentration of, 34
    sharing, 99
Weekend Edition Sunday (NPR),
    53
Welch, Jack, 67–68, 102

Western Europe, 62
why of life, 25
wildfires, 53
willpower, 27, 31, 35–36, 65–66, 93,
    100
windows of opportunity, 84
Winfrey, Oprah, 65
winning, xi–xii, 57–66
Win One for the Shareholders
    (Angrisani), xiv, 67, 81, 84, 86
win/win strategy, 87–95, 89–90, 91
Wooden, John, 102
WorldCom, 105
World War I, 12
World War II, 33, 46, 96, 123–24
worst-case scenarios, 93–94
writing, 21

Xbox, 85